TONY BENN has been Labour member of parliament for Bristol South-east since 1950, and currently serves on the Labour Party's national executive committee. His published writings include *The Regeneration of Britain* (1963), *Arguments for Socialism* (1979) and *Arguments for Democracy* (1981).

Tony Benn

Verso

Parliament, People and Power

Agenda for a Free Society

Interviews with New Left Review

This is an edited version of a series of
interviews conducted in London in March and June 1982.

The interviewers were members of the
New Left Review editorial committee

First published 1982
© Tony Benn and *New Left Review* 1982

Verso Editions and NLB
15 Greek Street, London W1

Typeset in Times by
Preface Ltd
Salisbury, Wilts.

Printed in Great Britain by
The Thetford Press Ltd
Thetford, Norfolk

ISBN 0-86091-057-1
ISBN 0-86091-758-4 Pbk

Contents

Foreword

A new socialist left has assembled in the Labour Party since the later seventies. Tony Benn is today the outstanding representative of this new force, and as such one of the most salient figures in the political upheavals of contemporary Britain.

The economic and social dimensions of the British crisis have been intensively debated in recent times, and never more so than in the past few years, with their background of deepening recession and ruthlessly imposed austerity. But the more distinctive features of the crisis in its current phase are specifically political: the convulsion of the parliamentary party order and the changing profile of the state itself.

The electoral defeat of the Callaghan government in 1979 triggered the fiercest inner-party controversy the Labour Party had known in decades. A new combination of the left resumed the struggle over policy, but this time fighting a parallel campaign for democratic accountability within the party, above all in its parliamentary sector. The early successes of this revitalized left provoked a fragment of the Labour right to secede and form a new party, the Social Democrats, whose alliance with the Liberals adumbrates a break in the established post-war pattern of political representation, with its dependable alternation of Conservative and Labour majorities. But the ultimate stakes in the twofold drive of the Labour left are the future of the Labour Party itself in its inherited form, and of socialist politics generally.

The context of these party disturbances was not only a deteriorating economic climate. Even as the Conservative government affected 'withdrawal' from the economy, deferring to 'market forces', the state was becoming a more palpable presence in British politics day to day. Callaghan's parliamentary downfall was itself shaped by the unresolved crisis in Northern Ireland and the bathetic outcome of the debate over Scottish and Welsh devolution. England's minority communities were no less disaffected than the minority nationalities of the 'United Kingdom', and two years later a chain of spontaneous riots dramatized the anger of black—but also white—youth at the treatment routinely meted out to them by the police and other state bodies. Externally, meanwhile, the British state assumed a forward role in the preparation of a new cold war, ordering the Trident weapons system and welcoming Cruise missiles as a necessary addition to NATO's already awesome local armoury. Domestic and international purposes were wedded in the Falklands war as Thatcher, proclaiming the rebirth of British pride and unwrapping a lethal array of modern weaponry, dispatched a naval task force to recover a tiny colonial possession whose British title the foreign office itself neither trusted nor valued. The state—its territorial extent, its domestic functioning, its international role—is now an issue in British politics, and thus a factor of disruption in the political order, above all in the Labour Party.

New Left Review has sought, over the years, to analyse and intervene in the course of British political and cultural debate, both in its own pages and in the more amplified form of book publication. Collections such as *Towards Socialism* (1965), *The Incompatibles: Trade-Union Militancy and the Consensus* (1967), *Student Power* (1969), and the interviews with Raymond Williams, *Politics and Letters* (1979), are instances of the latter. In the past two years the journal has likewise attempted systematic discussion of the political issues animating the British left today. Debate over the significance of the nuclear arms race was initiated by Edward Thompson (NLR 121) and continued by Raymond Williams, Roy and Zhores Medvedev, and Lucio Magri, and has now been published, greatly expanded, as *Exterminism and Cold War* (Verso/NLB 1982). The war for the Falklands is the subject of a special issue of the Review (Anthony Barnett's

'Iron Britannia', NLR 134). Meanwhile, the state and prospects of the Labour Party have been analysed variously by Michael Rustin, David Coates, Tom Nairn, Ken Coates, Tariq Ali, Quintin Hoare, and Geoff Hodgson (NLR 126, 129, 130, 131, 132, 133 respectively), in a continuing series.* The decision to conduct an extended interview with Tony Benn was an integral part of these linked editorial projects.

Tony Benn was among the first to call for greater democracy in the Labour Party; and through his remarkable campaign for the deputy leadership, which won overwhelming support in the constituency branches, he has become in effect a public symbol of the unfinished struggle for a party accountable to its committed rank and file. After the electoral defeat of 1970, he emerged as a candid critic of the Wilson administration and an ally of the stormy working-class resistance to the Heath government. Today he is the main proponent of a radical course for Labour, both within the party—defending the 1982 draft programme in the national executive committee—and more widely—playing a prominent role in the mobilizations for nuclear disarmament and in the movement against the expedition to the South Atlantic. The flair and determination of Benn's recent political activity have won the admiration of some of Labour's sternest revolutionary critics. As Paul Foot wrote: 'I found Tony Benn's summer and autumn campaign . . . exhilarating. He was talking socialism in terms at once more easy to understand and more powerful than anything which had come out of the Labour left in my adult life. And the result was to electrify the political scene. Interest in politics on the left soared. Mass meetings of the most extraordinary size and enthusiasm were staged . . . all over the country.'†

Benn's political views have become steadily more radical over the past decade—an evolution that his right-wing critics

---

*See too Eric Hobsbawm and others, *The Forward March of Labour Halted?*, Verso/NLB in association with *Marxism Today*, 1981.
†*Three Letters to a Bennite*, London 1982.

(though not only they) have queried. Yet his central and most novel political distinction has been constant over at least as many years. Unusually in the Labour Party, and uniquely among his parliamentary colleagues, Benn has focused sharply and insistently on the structures of the British state as obstacles or potential means to democratic government. No one in a comparable position has turned so searching an eye on the British constitution and its relation to the supposedly consensual ideal of democracy or the underlying reality of a capitalist social order. This central emphasis on the state as a strategic problem is unwonted not only in the Labour Party but also in the world-view of its sister parties in Europe and beyond. It constitutes the fundamental originality of Benn's politics.

These interviews were designed to furnish a synoptic, critical survey of Benn's political thought—his development, his current stance and perspectives—in relation both to the Labour Party and to the general position and prospects of socialism in Britain. Socialism has always encompassed a plurality of traditions marked by deep and lasting differences of strategic outlook. *New Left Review* has worked in the tradition of revolutionary socialism directly descended from Marx; Tony Benn's contrasting estimate of this tradition is set down in his Marx Memorial Lecture, 1981.‡ However, we share the view that this pluralism of the left can and should be turned to creative account in open and comradely debate framed by the common purpose of overcoming the power of capital and creating a socialist society. Some of the differences between Benn and NLR, in matters of general analysis, expectation and objective, and over particular questions of policy, are explored in what follows here. These discussions are scarcely definitive in range, let alone in the detail of the positions jointly or opposedly maintained. They are offered as a contribution to any

‡Now published as 'Democracy and Marxism: a Mutual Challenge', *Marxism Today*, May 1982.

agenda concerned with the paths of socialist politics in Britain, whether inside, outside or beyond the Labour Party, in the testing years ahead of us all.

NLR

1
A Political Journey

How would you describe your general political outlook in the period from 1950, when you entered parliament, to the eve of the 1964 general election?

To understand that you have to go back further. I was brought up in the household of a Labour MP, and therefore the thirties, when I was between five and fifteen, were one long family discussion of politics – issues like Spain and Abyssinia, the Japanese invasion of China, the rise of Hitler and so on. Besides, my father came from an old radical dissenting tradition and my mother was, and is, a student of theology, and this made the discussion of ideas and religion and politics very close. Then I went to university, and from there into the RAF. I had joined the Labour Party on the birthday when I became eligible, and I came back at the end of the war with my views deepened by – I suppose – the influences that made returning servicemen vote Labour, and strongly supported the new Labour government. During the war I had been interested in Common Wealth because I was opposed to the electoral truce, but of course I never joined that party (though I corresponded as a student with Richard Acland who was then involved in it). After leaving the services, I returned to university, eventually arriving at the House of Commons in 1950, just less than a year before the post-war Labour government was defeated.

It looked at that time as though the economic problems that had brought such a huge Labour majority were to some extent proving to be soluble. There were shortages and other difficulties, but I think a lot of people felt, and even at that stage I would have begun to feel, that the more radical socialist measures we had been discussing earlier might not have been so necessary. I did not concern myself with economic or industrial matters at the beginning. In those early years I was probably a pretty ordinary, run-of-the-mill Labour MP concerned with civil liberties, with the colonial freedom movement (I was very interested in that), with libertarian issues generally, and with the media – I worked with the BBC and one of my first speeches, in 1951 I think, was on the future role of the BBC. I served for ten years in the House of Commons before the peerage issue led to my exclusion. In that period I was made a front-bench defence spokesman; and in 1959 I was appointed shadow minister of transport. I got involved in industrial policy for the first time in that capacity. I would have regarded myself as radical then, but I did not join the Bevan group – though I was invited to do so – because I felt that a left that isolated itself from the mainstream of the party would weaken its own influence.

The Fifties Debates: Bevan and Gaitskell

But you seem to have developed quite early on a set of interests that were not at all particularly run-of-the-mill in the Labour Party at the time, focusing very much on the institutions of the British state. Your concern with the reform of parliament, with the civil service, seems to have been quite untypical of either the right or the left of the party. At the same time, the years immediately after you entered parliament were ones of extraordinary intense and acrimonious debate between right and left on economic issues, culminating at the end of the decade in the attempt to liquidate Clause Four. Did you really feel this was an irrelevant debate? After all, it was actually more alive after 1951, because the issues had exploded into the movement itself.

The two points are related. The issues that most concerned me then, and still concern me – democratic institutions versus the power of the secret police, the civil service, the military, and so on – have now become much more controversial, and indeed central, in the argument in the Labour Party. But at that time they were seen as marginal, and to that extent I was regarded as being out of the main stream. I was not really involved in the argument about Bevan's critique of Gaitskell's budget and the reintroduction of the Health Service charges and the rest. I had a radical instinct in support of what Bevan was saying, and, as I mentioned, was invited to join his group. But I did not engage in those central arguments. Even when it came to nuclear disarmament – a similarly divisive issue – my entry into it was on the grounds of public accountability rather than the straight question of unilateralism.

One very clear strand in your politics at the time was a passionate identification with the cause of colonial freedom; you were very militantly engaged over Suez, for instance. Now, for many who became involved at this point, Suez led very quickly and directly to CND; the two things were seen as being interlinked. It is clear that you already felt strongly about the dangers of nuclear weapons, yet it seems that on the whole you leant to Bevan's 1957 position in support of keeping the British bomb for purposes of international negotiation. You didn't actually join CND in 1958 though you resigned as spokesman for air over the policy of massive nuclear retaliation — and in 1959, and again at the Scarborough conference of 1960, you essentially supported Gaitskell's platform, while deploring the divisive way in which it was implemented and resigning from the national executive. Could you give us the background to your thinking at that time?

I was very deeply engaged over Suez. When Gaitskell made his speech on 2 August 1956 supporting Eden's position, I went with a delegation to see him and we brought him back, I thought, from the brink. I wrote with other MPs to Ben Gurion about the Israeli role and got a very bitter letter back; and I wrote to *Pravda* with others about the invasion of Hungary. That concurrence of issues involved me very actively – I spoke in Trafalgar Square, and so on. As for the nuclear issues, my first involvement in that was when I tried to put down a question about nuclear weapons, having discovered that the Labour government had built the atomic bomb without telling parliament. I was sternly rebuked by Attlee, which at the time was quite frightening, I being a new member and he a former prime minister and the party leader. Gaitskell put me on the front bench in 1956 – my first appointment – as a second defence, air, spokesman; I resigned a year later because I was not prepared to support the first use of nuclear weapons by Britain. Prior to that, I had been involved in setting up the Hydrogen Bomb National Committee. This was not specifically unilateralist; it was an attempt to see nuclear weapons as a problem of foreign policy. The campaign did not go very well; it culminated in the presentation of a petition at 10 Downing Street in December 1954. It later led to CND, however, and at that time I felt that British renunciation of nuclear weapons would not of itself contribute to the solution of the problem. This was quite different from Bevan's view, which I never shared, that we needed nuclear weapons to negotiate.

At the 1960 conference, when the clash between Gaitskell and Frank Cousins really developed, I felt – as I felt even more strongly over the Clause Four issue later – that the right was simply using nuclear weapons to cleanse the party of its left. I went to see both Gaitskell and Cousins to try to bring about a reconciliation. It was perhaps a foolhardy thing for a young MP to do. Gaitskell was so violent in his condemnation of Frank Cousins – using the sort of language he used in his Stalybridge speech, talking about 'fellow travellers, nonentities, cranks. . . .'. He absolutely rejected my efforts. Then I went to see Cousins, who thought I had come as a representative of Gaitskell, and I had a similarly rough time from him! I concluded that the nuclear issue was being used as an excuse for a split on the part of the right, and that was when I broke with Gaitskell. I voted for Wilson in the subsequent leadership elections, but I lost my commons seat almost immediately afterwards, when my father died, and when I came back in 1963 Wilson was already leader of the party. So my interpretation of my position would be that – clearly – I was slow to see unilateralism as contributing to the anti-nuclear case worldwide, but not slow to see the importance of parliamentary control over nuclear weapons, and the relationship of this to foreign policy. I did not argue for unilateralism until the cabinet discussed nuclear weapons in 1974.

How did you see Gaitskell? Your perception must have changed over the years. . . .

First of all, I think my view of him was shaped by my having been elected at the end of the 1945 Labour government and seeing it break up before my very eyes. I was present at one parliamentary party meeting in 1951, when Bevan and Morrison clashed openly. It was like being present at an earthquake. I was sorry that Bevan resigned in 1951, in part because of the effect on the general election prospects – and we were defeated in October 1951. At that time I would have been hoping that he could have carried on.

My assessment of Gaitskell was based partly on the fact that he had certain radical instincts. He was quite good on Africa, for example, and on racial matters – on the immigration legislation – certainly better than some other right-wing leaders we've had. He had, as we now know, a very strong instinctive opposition to the Common Market, which led him once to describe Roy Jenkins to me as an 'extremist', meaning somebody who was pro-Common Market! These were some of the qualities about Gaitskell that I found agreeable. I worked with him very closely on all his party broadcasts. At the time of Suez he made a party political broadcast as leader, and I spent the whole day helping him to draft his statement, in which he said that Labour would support another Tory leader if they'd stop the war. This pledge caused a tremendous sensation at the time. The moment of my break with Gaitskell came over nuclear weapons and over his determination to change Clause Four in 1960. Although he had accepted my help, I was never really trusted because I kept raising difficult questions which he regarded as either irrelevant or somehow too radical. Gaitskell was someone who thought you were either with him or against him: he could never see shades of opinion. That is the way I saw him in the end.

Renouncing the Peerage

Between 1960 and 1963 you fought what was obviously a very formative struggle to renounce your peerage, standing for your Bristol constituency in defiance of what was then the constitutional status quo. This seems to be one of the very few instances, if the record is right, where on a basic issue of democratic rights the whole of the Labour party did more or less stand behind you.

That's not quite right. I'm not making any complaint, but in fact some Labour MPs thought, 'This is irrelevant, it's not a trade-union issue. Here is a privileged young man, who has been in parliament for ten years. His father took a peerage – all right, he was Labour but he took a peerage – and now this young man loses his seat in the House and wants us to save him.' There was not much sympathy in the party for Hailsham ten years earlier when he inherited a peerage – I think rightly not, because Hailsham wanted to remain a peer *and* be in the Commons, and Attlee would not have it. Had there been a Labour government in 1960 when my father died, I would not have been helped at all; of that I am absolutely certain. But there was also a lot of support from the grassroots of the party, a lot of public support, and there were some members of the parliamentary party who were immensely helpful. Charlie Pannell, for instance: he was a right-wing AUEW MP, but he took up the case as an issue of personal liberty. Gaitskell was quite helpful too. Considering I had just voted against him in the 1960 leadership election, it was very good of him to reappoint me to the front bench and retain me as shadow transport minister when I was actually not in the House of Commons. He kept me as spokesman until the end of 1960, when it became absolutely obvious that he had to find a replacement, and he gave me strong support in the House. George Brown, by contrast, was very hostile, although he came down to Bristol to speak in the by-election.

The case had a strange effect: it produced a lot of public support; it divided radicals from, if you like, the non-radical element of the parliamentary party, and I can't blame them for not regarding it as central. It also drew support from outside the Labour Party – Churchill, Edward Boyle, Jo Grimond, and so on – and that worried some Labour people. But Nye Bevan did sign the instrument of renunciation, which was one of the propaganda devices. Bevan, Grimond, Julian Amery, all signed it: quite an interesting sheet of paper! The Labour Party stuck by me, but at the end, when I was defeated, I was summoned to see Ray Gunter, who was then the chairman of the organization committee of the party. He told me that in no circumstances whatever, if the man who had beaten me, Malcolm St. Clair, resigned, would the party support me in a second election. And Gaitskell suggested that my wife, Caroline, stand as a candidate – a ludicrous idea that incensed both me and her. It was a typical British device, you know, 'You've made your point, now quieten down' – which is the way the left had been diverted century after century. In the end, of course, the victory went rather sour and became a farce, because Home took advantage of it, as did Hailsham, the 1963 Tory leadership crisis. But at the time it was a genuine radical struggle that attracted the support of a lot of very good people, though by no means all the PLP.

You say 'a farce', but the irony is that you were directly responsible for Lord Home's becoming prime minister.

That's what the Tories said in order to laugh off what had been a very serious defeat for the Establishment. In 1950 you could not get into the House of Lords unless you were a man and unless you had been created a hereditary peer or had inherited a title, and you could not leave in any circumstances. After the 1958 Life Peerages Act – which was partly enacted to avoid the problems I had raised – and the Peerage Act which allowed renunciation, the law was transformed. Now people enter the Lords by appointment for life or may resign on inheritance; and women can sit in it. Moreover, the creation of hereditary peers has effectively ended.

On the other hand, the House of Lords is now a very much more dangerous organization, because it has been made respectable by these reforms in its composition. At the time the struggle was bitter, and when I re-read the speeches made in opposition to this modest change I am reminded that only twenty-five years ago there really was an absolutely feudal attitude to the parliamentary system. The Judges and the Election Court threw me out of the Commons on the basis of a single ruling by Mr Justice Dodderidge in 1626, which held that a peerage was an 'incorporeal hereditament affixed to the blood and annexed to the posterity'. On the basis of that phrase my constituents were denied their elected MP. It was an amazing battle, lasting ten years, from 1953 to 1963.

Wasn't Butler at the time especially intransigent?

His handling of the issue destroyed his liberal image. Butler found the whole episode acutely embarassing, but the government would not budge and Butler was the man who had to get up in the Commons and say: 'Not only will we throw Mr Benn out, we will not even give him a hearing first.' This did considerable damage to his reputation. In the end, as the Tories always do when the game is not worth the candle, they gave way on the minor thing in order to preserve their real interest – in this case the House of Lords itself.

Labour in Government 1964 – 70

Let's turn now to the Wilson administration, which was your own first direct experience of government. You made a speech in 1972 in which you said, speaking of the administration as a whole: 'History will be much more generous about our achievements than are our critics.' After the six years of government, what were your immediate reflections on the experience; and how would you judge the record of those years today?

I would divide them into different periods. I returned to the House in October 1963, and in the year leading up to the election I really did believe that we had found a very much better leader in Wilson. He had identified the scientific theme, which was important. He wasn't saying that science would produce miracles; rather that if you hadn't ever had socialism before, the scientific revolution would make socialist planning necessary. When he talked about 'the white heat of the technological revolution', he was really talking about the effect of this on human beings. With massive investment in new technology, people would be sacked. That was the white heat – a sort of furnace which was going to recast the whole of our economic and industrial system. In justice to him, at the time he did inspire the Labour Party. He had a broadly internationalist outlook and he had talked a lot about the importance of the United Nations, which attracted many people of my generation. As for myself, for the first eighteen months of government I was busy in the Post Office, which was, and still is, the fastest-growing technology-oriented industry in the country. I found that very interesting, especially the close links established with the trade unions. I established, a publicly-owned bank, which had long been an aspiration of the Union of Post Office Workers and others, set up the national data-

processing service, turned the Post Office into a public corporation, and tried to develop a more pluralistic broadcasting system. I was not in the cabinet, and hence out of the
main stream, but I had no general criticism of government
policy at that time.

That was 1964–66. Then came 1966–68, when I was
given what I would now call an 'SDP brief' in the ministry of
technology. The terms of the brief had already been set by
the victory of 1966, and the U-turn that took place after the
seamen's strike, on the eve of the July deflationary measures.
My brief from Wilson was to try to improve industrial performance by micro-economic measures such as mergers, as with
the Geddes Report on ship-building. For the next two years
(apart from being involved now for the first time in central
economic issues – in July 1966 I voted with a minority for
devaluation against deflation), I was involved in trying, as
best as I could, to pursue the sort of policies that were later
applied by Heath and then Varley – dirigiste policies now
espoused by the SDP. That was a very active period. But it
was then that my political position began to change, because
the more I saw of this process, the more I became convinced
(a) that it would not work, (b) that it was corporatist, and (c)
that it was anti-trade union and undemocratic. So, beginning
in January 1968 and continuing through the year, I made a
series of political speeches about the future of socialism. I
led a dual life from 1968 to 1970: continuing in the ministry
of technology as, I hoped, an efficient and hardworking
minister, and at the weekends publicly warning the party
that if we went along this route we were going to get into
difficulties.

That's when my conflict with Wilson began. He had been
very displeased that I voted for devaluation in 1966. But the
real conflicts, which became very intense, occurred between
1968 and 1970. I used to get warnings from him: I was not to
make speeches, all my speeches were to be vetted by Judith
Hart, who was then the minister responsible for information,
and so on. Then in 1970, after our defeat, I wrote a pamphlet,
The New Politics – a Socialist Reconnaissance, in which I

tried to put the experience and lessons of office together. When I said in 1972 that history would be more generous to the 1964 – 70 Labour government, it was because I was anxious not to repudiate entirely the record of the government of which I had been a member. I would say the same, in certain circumstances, about the 1974 – 79 Labour government. I think history *will* be more generous than some critics were. Those governments did some useful things better than their predecessors or successors. But I did not want to give the impression that for the trade unions to come back into partnership with the Labour Party on a new basis it was necessary for *them* to repudiate the entire experience of Labour in office, though I also made clear that the next Labour government would have to be different.

Were you saying to the TUC: the defeat in 1970 was the responsibility not just of the Labour government but also of the unions, who had failed to educate their membership and to play a much more forward cultural and political role?

I was saying that they gave the impression of being concerned exclusively with wages, of being too non-political a movement; that the row between us had gone on for a couple of years now, and really it was time to pull together again. That's the sort of speech it was intended to be.

Deflation, Devaluation, and the Unions

Both within the cabinet and within the leadership of the Labour Party, the famous July 1966 measures created mixed sets of forces in which there was no clear left-right division. Some right-wing figures — Brown, for instance, and Crosland — argued for devaluation, as you did, while Barbara Castle would probably have supported Wilson. How did you perceive the issue at the time?

The decision to abandon the 1964 national plan in favour of deflation seemed to a lot of us, including myself, to be a return to the old stop-go policy. I can't say I believed then that devaluation would do the trick – though I did argue for it consistently when I was in the inner cabinet and we did decide to devalue, about a year afterwards. But in 1966 it was clear that deflation involved the destruction of the whole planning revival we had introduced with the establishment of the department of economic affairs. I was up at the Durham Miners' Gala with George Brown – it was the night before Wilson flew to Moscow – and Brown said to me: 'I am resigning, this is the end, the whole thing is finished.' Remember, at that time he was seen as an industrial planning minister whose job was to break the power of the Treasury. There was a lot of sympathy with him just then. The following day he spoke to Wilson – at the airport, I think – and the result was that he stayed in the cabinet, resigning from the DEA and moving to the Foreign Office. What happened was that the subsequent deflation destroyed the possibility of running even an SDP-type industrial policy. Wilson's alternative was to go for secret reflation through micro-measures of industrial investment. That was when we got the Industrial Reorganization Bill through, and the Industrial Expansion Bill. A lot of micro-investment was envisaged, which was intended to avoid the effects of old-style deflation. A year later we went for devaluation, but even that did not really solve the problem: there were cuts upon cuts after the 1967 devaluation, because there was no way we could manipulate ourselves out of the central economic squeeze.

The second such episode, which also had serious, probably decisive, consequences for the Labour government, centred on the scheme for trade-union law reform, In Place of Strife. *Again the lines of division were rather confused: Callaghan seems to have been the main opponent of the scheme, while Barbara Castle, on the left, was the main proponent. . . .*

That's right. I was not involved in the early discussions about *In Place of Strife*. The policy implied two things: first, you can't run the system with full employment unless you get trade-union power under control; and secondly, a political strategy that was pure self-deception for a Labour party: that it was possible to rise above politics and so become 'the natural party of government'. The theory was that having won power on the backs of the trade unions, we could say to the electorate, 'We are no longer under the influence of trade unions'. This was extraordinary; but for a time I went along with it. There were some people who knew about trade unionism, including Dick Marsh and James Callaghan, on the right, who were very critical of the scheme. The trade unions themselves were divided about it. There were some leaders who were quite happy to see it happen because it would control their rank and file, but would not say so publicly; there were others who were totally committed against it. When we reached an impasse from which there was no possible escape except war with the movement or capitulation, I came out very strongly for dropping it. But I do not come out of that episode very well; my judgement was totally wrong, and I can now see that this was the second stage of revisionism in the party. Gaitskell had wanted to get rid of socialism by dropping Clause Four; Wilson wanted to break our links with the unions. I was slow to understand the danger of what was proposed

So were the line-ups, in your view, essentially ad hoc, *or were you conscious of any developing left-right division in this period?*

The devaluation issue was really seen as an argument about what one would call economic management: would you or would you not do better by trying to hold the value of the pound, which Wilson as an economic nationalist was very keen to do. I believe that Balogh and Kaldor had actually written a paper on devaluation while the government was busy with the 1966 elections, and that when Wilson heard of it he had every copy burnt. That was the story, and I believe it. Devaluation had become a taboo subject, and of course

Callaghan, like every chancellor, felt he had to defend the currency. The cabinet decision not to devalue in July 1966 was seen as 'a vote of confidence' in Harold Wilson. I must mention this because it is highly relevant to what I now believe about cabinet government. In every key argument in which I was ever involved, a majority was obtained for the prime minister's own view, which was always presented as a question of a vote of confidence in him personally, and this continued right up to the end of the Callaghan government. Too many votes of confidence destroy the power of cabinets to decide democratically on the merits of a case. I took the view that deflation would involve the destruction of the national plan, and you could argue that it was a a left-right division to that extent but it was more than that. Now, the second issue revealed some very complicated motivations. I believe that one of the reasons why Wilson and Castle were keen on *In Place of Strife* was to settle old scores with the trade-union leaders who had oppressed the left in the 1950s. Another motive was the desire to rise above politics. And the third factor, which was and still is very clearly identifiable, was this: unless you do concede to labour its rightful position in society, which means socialist reform, you are driven into a position where you are always fighting labour. Once we had closed the socialist option we had to resort to a pay policy, *In Place of Strife*, and so on. The wage-restraint option led us to defeat in 1970 – as it did Heath in 1974 and Callaghan in 1979. But in their own terms, Castle and Wilson did grasp that something had to be done to deal with the economic problem. Unfortunately their policy made the working class pay for the crisis.

Now, the opposition to *In Place of Strife* was partly that of right-wingers who had spent their lives in the trade-union movement; they were not prepared to see it crushed by a Labour government in whatever cause; and they believed, quite correctly too, that the movement had a life distinct from the party, for Labour would not always be in office, and there would have to be a trade-union movement in periods of opposition. That was the Callaghan-and-Marsh position, which was strongly reinforced in the House of Commons and of course in the trade-union movement. In retrospect, it was a highly significant episode, which greatly humiliated the prime minister. The defeat of *In Place of Strife* really established that the labour movement, when it had an absolutely fundamental interest to defend, could not be cajoled and bullied by an elected government, even a Labour government, and that was very important. The defeat also raised the question of whether Wilson could resolve his problem by calling an election. It was made absolutely clear to him that if he went to the Palace and resigned, somebody else would be in a taxi two minutes later, and would point out that our commons majority was so huge that Labour could form a government under a new leader if need be. So the interconnected issues of prime-ministerial power and the role of the Crown in agreeing to a dissolution, could have come to the forefront as well.

Vietnam and Rhodesia

There is a third crux in the record of this government, concerning foreign policy. Of all the shortcomings of the 1964–70 administration, the most lamentable lay here. Above all there was Wilson's refusal to take any distance from the American war in Vietnam, and secondarily, though in some respects even more culpably, there was a complete failure to do anything about Rhodesia, which was actually in the government's own bailwick. These issues must surely have concerned you a lot, given your early and continuing solidarity with anti-colonial struggles. How were such issues handled, and what were your own feelings at the time?

You must remember that for the first two years after 1964 I was still not a member of the cabinet. After that, I was watching what was happening in Vietnam and anxious about it, but I did not contribute very much in cabinet on the question of the British relationship with US policy, and it was not often discussed. On Rhodesia, which was discussed

much more often, I did feel incensed, though the main decision – against the use of force – had been taken before I
joined the cabinet, after UDI in October 1965. Another
decision, which I was unaware of until the Bingham report,
on oil supplies to Ian Smith, was published, was that anything we did about Rhodesia should fall short of confrontation with South Africa. But there was only one discussion,
after I joined the cabinet, about the use of force against
Rhodesia. I certainly felt that in ruling out intervention to
secure African rights, the government had actually handed
victory on a plate to Ian Smith who indeed retained power
until he was forced to give way under the pressure of the
liberation struggle.

On the Rhodesian question, I was more active in argument than I was on Vietnam, although I opposed the war. I
was also, engaged in one area of foreign policy which
occupied a great deal of my time, and which I still feel was
greatly worthwhile: and that was developing, under the
umbrella of technology, a whole series of agreements with
Eastern Europe. I went to the Soviet Union several times,
signed agreements with the Russians, with the Hungarians;
went to Yugoslavia, talked to the Czechs, and so on. During
that period I was deliberately trying to use technological
cooperation as a means of easing Cold War pressures. The
huge gas pipeline that is now being run into Western Europe
from Russia, and which so upsets the Americans, is very
much a product of that approach.

*Were international questions completely marginal in cabinet
discussion, then?*

Yes. In all the cabinets I have served in there have always
been three wholly unreformed departments: the Treasury,
the Home Office and the Foreign Office. Whereas no other
cabinet minister can do anything controversial without
explicit consent from the cabinet – a paper is put in, there is
a debate, the prime minister sums up, and the whole thing is
decided – the foreign secretary normally reported orally

under one item on the agenda: 'Oversea Affairs'. The foreign secretary would report every week, but there was no collective control whatever over foreign policy. Similarly, there was no collective control over the budget, which is the central economic judgement of the year. The Home Office operated over large areas of policy – as in security matters – largely by prerogative, so that was never discussed. When you look at cabinet government, you will find that on many crucial questions there is no real discussion. I involved myself very much more directly – this was the 1974 – 79 Labour government – in the Common Market debate, which, of course involved foreign policy. I put in rival papers to the chancellor on economic policy – these were permitted but not welcomed, and then were not always circulated. Home Office matters, like the Agee and Hosenball case, were never discussed. Now, if you add to that absolutely critical and structural problem of what I would call cabinet as distinct from parliamentary government the tendency to departmentalize ministers, you find that cabinets don't really govern the country. The Irish question, for example, was never properly discussed by the last Labour cabinet at all. There was a Northern Ireland Committee but we never had real discussion about major options on Ireland. I did, at the end of the 1974 – 79 government, write a minute to the prime minister asking for a cabinet discussion on Ireland. But it was not put on the agenda. Apart from the limited scope for individual ministers, where I see a lot I would have done differently, there are structural defects in cabinet government, which contribute to an acceptance of policies that really ought to have been identified as centrally important and argued out with passion and feeling, as other matters were during that period.

Reconsiderations

Two questions, then, about the general nature of this administration. One is, if you like, the socialist question; the other might be asked by a socialist or by a capitalist. First, why in

*your view did the radical promise of the administration fade
so quickly and completely after 1965? Second, why did it fail
so completely even as a project of capitalist modernization?
The latter question touches directly on your own tenure in
Mintech. After all, this was the period of great mergers, of
state-sponsored industrial concentration, which was designed
to rationalize the economy. But the results were minimal.*

To look back on that period and comment on it in the light
of what we know now is to take unfair advantage of hind-
sight, I think. I'm not sure that what I am about to say I
would have said then, so I've got to be very careful. In 1964
the theme of modernization, of science, of better planning,
of a radical Britain, was such an enormous improvement
over the Gaitskell years that it was seen by a lot of people as
a re-run of 1945. And it was, in its own terms, very radi-
cal.Immediately we came in the pressures were put on us,
and we were wholly unprepared for them. The ' Brown
Paper', as it was called, published in November 1964, was
the beginning of the attempt to control public expenditure
and resist the pressure of the bankers. By the summer of
1966 that attempt had failed. After that we were trying to
manage defensively. From 1966 onwards policy was really
the product of the narrowing range of options available to a
government not prepared to tackle fundamental questions. I
don't think I fully understood that at the time. I thought that
if you worked hard enough it would come right. Of course it
did not come right. And so we not only failed to achieve our
socialist objectives but saw the progressive relative weaken-
ing of the British economy and industrial base which made
us more vulnerable than any other industrialized country
when the 1973 oil price increases came along and triggered
off the events that led to the present depression. But if I had
been asked to make a critique of the experience, even as late
as 1970 my emphasis would have been on the undemocratic
nature of government decision-making, and on the failure to
do what might have been done, not on the fundamental
weakness of the policy. That understanding was just beginning.

You seem to see a wholesale regression of the Wilson government after 1966. But wasn't the foundation of the Open University a sign that at least some democratic and progressive potential remained?

Yes, and that's one reason why I said what I did in 1972. The Open University, which Wilson was extremely keen on, was a very positive achievement; it has had, I think, a profound effect on our educational capabilities. But without wanting to write off the whole experience, I'd come back to my point about democracy. I was thrown out of Wilson's kitchen cabinet, of which I had been a member since 1963, after a conflict with him over this question in 1968. He said, in a nutshell, that as he saw it, 'people want to go on playing cricket and let me run the country'. He really wanted a sort of socialist doctor's mandate. Perhaps because of his civil service background, or his liberal background, or whatever, Wilson was particularly hostile to all the democratic ideas I was airing. He sent me a warning message in 1968, after my speech on broadcasting, in which I had argued for public accountability in, and public access to, the media. 1971brought a complete break with him. I continued to work with him over a period after that, but the break had occurred, and it culminated, of course, in my dismissal from the department of industry in 1975.

This brings us back to the evolution of your own thinking in office. You've periodized both the course of the government and the shifts in your political outlook very clearly. But the public record appears in some respects discrepant with your interpretation. As late as 1967, for example, you made speeches lauding the mixed economy. You said: 'In Britain we are working a mixed system, within which the frontiers of public and private enterprise will change and will be the subject of argument'. And then: 'Very few people will want to see this system fundamentally changed in one direction or the other.'

That was an accurate representation of the policy of the government of which I was a member. Within a year you will find speeches about the democratic themes which run absolutely counter to that. The dichotomy between the week-day minister and the socialist who's trying to think it out in weekend speeches later became very acute, a sort of crisis within my own mind. It was during this period that my socialism was emerging from experience. It wasn't clearly formulated did not have the class basis it later acquired, did not have the theoretical superstructure or historical sense that were needed to make it effective. I was locked into a heavy programme of daily business that made it very hard to do more than air my developing ideas to myself and to others. It was after the 1970 defeat that the outcome of that inner conflict began to take shape for me, in a clearer socialist perception.

In your Llandudno speech, made in May 1968 as it happens, you were saying that a cross on a ballot paper every five years is completely insufficient as a definition of democracy. It was a very radical speech.

Yes, but it was not until the 1970–74 period, when I was a shadow minister, that I was free to allow the weekend-speech analysis to come into the policy-making.

In Opposition 1970 – 74

Your public political postures seemed to radicalize quite rapidly in the period of opposition. In the light of what you've described could you say whether this radicalization was also in part a response to the UCS work-in, the Pentonville Five, and the industrial struggles of that period? Did you feel basically at one with the flow of party opinion, or not?

A number of factors were at work. First of all, there had been this feeling of disappointment in the government, which had been held in control by the need for loyalty. I would not call it 'collective cabinet responsibility', it was loyalty to a government and the desire not to open the way for the Tories. The second point, of course, was that events began to take hold in a very powerful way. There was the collapse of Rolls Royce, then UCS. In the course of all this a great deal came out that confirmed my own experience, and therefore I felt familiar with what was happening and was trying to develop the positive elements in the situation. The third thing was that in a shadow cabinet where you are elected, not appointed, your relationship with your colleagues changes. In the cabinet proper everyone is looking at the boss who can hire and fire them, but in the shadow cabinet everyone is elected and has his or her own PLP constituency. Therefore my conflicts with Wilson intensified. He was angry about my support for the UCS and various other things that I did, and absolutely furious about my support for the Pentonville Five, but there was nothing much he could do about it. So growing support in the labour movement allowed me to try to put into practice the ideas I had been developing in government. I suppose the movement as a whole had that pent-up feeling too. It had been equally contained by loyalty when Labour was in power, and there was probably a general sense of release corresponding to my own. Not all members of the PLP were pleased by what I was doing, particularly in relation to the EEC referendum initiative, and support for direct action.

Two rather contradictory themes appeared in your speeches in this period. On one occasion, at the end of the Wilson government, you claimed that by and large it would be a great mistake to think that Labour cabinets were not closely in touch with the feeling of the party's rank and file. Yet in your Fabian Lecture of 1971, you singled out, very clearly and self-critically, at least five major areas where you said the movement had been right and the Labour government wrong. Vietnam, In Place of Strife, East of Suez, prescription charges and devaluation — a pretty comprehensive list. Were you already trying to work towards an alternative politics for the next Labour government?

But both themes were valid. The important aspect of the lecture was that it began to identify party democracy as a crucial issue. I didn't come up with a solution, but at least I was identifying a key question. When I look back on it now, that speech was very modest. It came in the middle of the deputy leadership election, in which I was a candidate, running against Jenkins. The constituency for the deputy leadership then was the PLP, and a lot of the speech was about the way the PLP was structured and on its relationship to the rank and file.

One very concrete outcome of the line of argument you started to develop in 1968 was your initiative for a referendum on the EEC. How was that received?

Initially there was no support whatever. I found myself in a minority of one both in the shadow cabinet and on the national executive. The proposal became bitterly controversial within the PLP, though the movement outside accepted it quickly.

So even the left in the NEC did not initially welcome the idea at all?

No, they did not.

Was all the opposition on the conventional grounds that this has got nothing to do with the way we British understand the sovereignty of parliament?

Jenkins, for example, compared the idea with plebiscites and authoritarian government, and claimed it was divisive. But when I first raised it in the shadow cabinet in November 1970 Jim Callaghan said at the close of the discussion – no doubt it was these qualities that led him to the premiership – 'Well, at least we must thank Tony for launching a little rubber dinghy into which one day we may all wish to clamber'.

It was rather like the peerage case, which had begun as a great radical battle and ended up as something convenient for the establishment. The referendum began as, and was intended to be, a radical initiative, and ended up as a little rubber dinghy into which the Labour cabinet did indeed clamber. (It was the shadow cabinet's final acceptance of the idea that precipitated Jenkins's resignation.) The dinghy then scuppered itself, of course, when the Labour cabinet came out by a majority in favour of renegotiated terms. This initiative represented my break with what I would call the inner-parliamentary, the *parliamentarian* view of politics – a break that had actually begun with the peerage episode, when I discovered that there was a thing called parliamentarianism that had nothing whatever to do with democracy. Parliamentarianism is the disease that has infected the Labour Party. It is not parliamentary democracy in a proper sense, but the idea that when you have elected MPs they join a little club of people who know better than everyone else. That's why those five examples in the 1971 lecture incensed the PLP: they revealed a widely held view that wisdom was not disclosed solely to the cabinet, indeed quite the opposite. The party was usually well ahead of events, and I still believe that most strongly.

Economic Policy and Party Democracy

Two of the most burning issues confronting the labour movement today were first posed in this period. One, as you say, is inner-party democracy. To what extent were you consciously taking up demands that were already being articulated by the activists from below?

The Campaign for Labour Party Democracy was actually formed in May 1973, after the Churchill Hotel NEC, at which Wilson vetoed the commitment to nationalize twenty-five companies.

So your initiative preceded that in the party itself?

Only by a little: the Tribune group was working on the issue at about the same time.

*The way in which you broached this question is rather curious
— and not uncharacteristic. To put it very summarily, you
make an extremely radical critique of the existing state of
affairs, but then are studiously vague about the remedy. You
say, for example, 'We should resist the temptation to propose
some obvious ways in which the democratic pressures within
the Labour party could be considerably reinforced. . . .' And
again, '. . . . It would be a great mistake to start this debate by
looking for precise solutions to problems of democratic
responsibilities that have not yet been properly analysed and
considered'. What prompted this style of intervention?*

At the time this was held to be a radical speech, and I had
two thoughts in mind in drafting it. First of all, if I'd come up
with specific solutions it would have been easy to shoot them
down. You only have to look at the debate over the many
variants of electoral college to see what an argument there
might have been, and its probable outcome. I was trying to
get these very explosive ideas on to the agenda without
exposing myself to a whole range of objections to the effect
that my proposals were impractical.

The second point was that I was immensely conscious of
the fact, and my whole political life since the peerage case
has borne this out, that you can never win a battle inside
until you've actually stimulated a discussion and mobilized
opinion outside. The belief that all change comes from outside entails opening up the argument so that people outside
can begin pressing, and then you can assist them from inside.
I have done this over a long period – the recent commons bill
making nuclear bases illegal is a case in point. It is what I call
'smuggling messages out of prison'. This procedure may
sound strange but it is the way in which the people who are
near the top – which I suppose I am – can contribute and act
constructively with people outside who know that something
is wrong but don't have the confidence to press for reform. It
is a view of how the parliamentary process properly works,
based on the belief that all change comes from below.

The second urgent question is that of the Alternative

Economic Strategy. At the Blackpool Conference in 1973, talking about future economic strategy, you said very clearly that the next Labour government would inherit a tremendous economic crisis, which should be seen as an opportunity not simply to patch up capitalism but to change it. Thus the phrase about an 'irreversible shift in the balance of wealth and power', which was much noticed in the press at the time. Yet in the same speech you fended off a demand for the national-ization of the 250 largest companies, a demand to which sec-tions of the Labour Party are still attached today. Then, in presenting the new policy to the press, you actually sidestep-ped the more modest commitment to 25 companies. You did this in a radical way, it's true, saying that if the Heath gov-ernment had already nationalized 27 companies, why should Labour get fixated on just 25. But do you think now, on looking back, that it was wise to dissociate the general objec-tive, which you posed very clearly and eloquently, from specific actual commitments — in the light of what actually happened afterwards?

Your question in fact refers in several episodes and issues that came up in 1973. One turning point came on the home policy committee that year, when we were trying to formu-late a new policy. Just putting public ownership back on the agenda was immensely radical – it still is – and I remember Callaghan saying, in effect, 'Oh, we can't do that'. I argued that we had to aim for some big objective, for a 'fundamen-tal and irreversible shift of wealth and power in favour of working people', and managed to incorporate that general commitment in the 1973 programme – it has remained, and appears in the 1982 programme.

The second issue arose at the Churchill Hotel. Judith Hart's industrial policy working group had come up with the proposal to nationalize 25 companies, and this was carried by a majority of one at the end of the day. Wilson immedi-ately declared that he had a veto. I did not then want, any more than I want now, the arguments to be presented in such a way that the credibility of the programme as a whole came under attack. I said there need be no great emphasis on one number rather than another. Wilson, on the other hand, was determined to kill the specific proposal for nationalization; he spent the whole summer in the attempt and he came to the conference in October 1973 having succeeded.

Now, at the conference itself there were two events. The first was the resolution on 250 companies. That went beyond even what had been agreed in the Churchill Hotel, and I used the argument, which I think had a certain validity, that you should never nationalize anything without the consent of the people who work in the industry. Second, if you were really asking people to take on board a change of that kind without having thought out how you'd do it, you would encourage disappointment. That was the view that I put forward on behalf of the executive.

As for 'the crisis we inherit'. That phrase formed in my mind after Roy Jenkins had declared, though not in so many words, that the economic programme was all rubbish, because of course when we came to power there would be a crisis. I said, replying to the debate, that 'the crisis we inherit must be the occasion for radical change and not the excuse for postponing it'.

Those two phrases have become in a way symbolic of the change that occurred then. I recently attended a conference in Bristol about the Alternative Economic Strategy, and an old trade unionist I have known for years came up to me and said 'Surely the AES is what we agreed in 1973. What's the difference? I replied: 'There isn't any difference. It *is* what we said in 1973, but we never did it.' Just as – I believe – we won the 1945 election on the basis of the 1935 manifesto, so in effect the next election will be fought on the manifesto of 1974. But this time we must mean it. I believe there is a kind of ten-year cycle involved in all reforms. The party democracy proposal of 1971 was realized in 1981. If you look at the time-scale of radical change from below, it does take about ten years for the wisdom of the rank and file to filter through and be acted upon by those at the top.

Return to Government 1974 – 79

*When was the AES proper first conceived as a definite gov-
ernmental option?*

In January 1975. I submitted to the economic committee of
the cabinet a paper drafted by Francis Cripps which we had
discussed together with Eric Heffer, Michael Meacher and
Frances Morrell, and in which the options before us were
classified as 'strategy A' and 'strategy B'. That paper was the
beginning of the AES. Cripps was saying, if you go for
strategy A you will end up in a confrontation with the
trade-union movement and will be defeated; if you go for
strategy B, it will mean the following alternative course. In
the IMF discussions eighteen months later this choice
became one between the cuts and the full AES; the cabinet
stuck to strategy A and paved the way for our defeat in
1979.

*It is often said that it was a fatal tactical error on the part of the
left inside the party and the government to concentrate so
heavily on the EEC issue. The referendum defeat allowed
Wilson and the leadership to reconstruct the government very
radically, marginalizing you and effectively ditching the radical component of Labour's official programme.*

I don't entirely accept that. The EEC was the inevitable
focus for the debate as to whether we were to have a planned
economy or whether we were to abandon national planning
and submerge ourselves in the free movement of capital and
goods under the Treaty of Rome. Wilson was unquestion-
ably determined to take us into the Common Market. He
appointed a cabinet with an allegedly anti-Common Market
majority, but it included people who were not really serious
about their opposition. Wilson was very doubtful and pessimistic about the miners: the strike would cost us the election, he would lose a law-and-order contest, and so on. He
was very surprised when we won. However, he realised that
we would have to call a further election six months or so

later, and therefore he couldn't really disturb the balance within the cabinet until he had settled the European question in favour of entry. This meant that there was some tipping of the hat towards the programme of 1973, which some of us thought he did not believe in.

So throughout the summer of 1974 we had long arguments, the most exhausting and bitter disputes I have ever been involved in, over the White Paper on the regeneration of industry. Wilson took the chair himself in the end, because his views were losing out in committee. He announced endlessly that *he* was in charge. All this culminated in a series of meetings which I hope I never have to live through again. I simply took his speech from the 1973 conference, photocopied it and read it to him across the table. Remember that in 1973, having opposed the 25 companies proposal, he knew perfectly well that he had to make a very radical speech at the conference. And he did. It was the most radical speech I ever heard him give. So, in 1974 I quoted the words he had used. It was a bitter battle, and it resulted in a somewhat diluted White Paper. We had the second, October, election before the EEC renegotiation was over, and we won just marginally. *Still* Wilson could not make the disposition he wanted, removing me from Industry and changing the industrial policy – he had to keep the show on the road for the referendum.

So: we had an election victory in March on a more radical programme than the prime minister wanted, followed by a partially successful battle to water it down. Then we had the second election, on a weaker manifesto qualified by the White Paper. Wilson had to live through another six months before the renegotiation came back to cabinet in March 1975. But then he completed his hat-trick with a third election – because that's what the referendum was – in which the Labour Party and the labour movement were defeated, while his Labour government remained in power. After that he moved with tremendous speed. The way was then clear for the winding up of the industrial policy, and there was a Chequers meeting in November 1974, which I was forced to attend as a sort of captive and watch the whole thing being reversed.

But I don't believe that if we had focused on that rather than on the EEC question, which had to be resolved anyway, we would have gained any advantage. What is true, however, is that the referendum defeat frightened the trade-union leaders into believing that the government was only hanging on by the skin of its teeth; and the economic crisis following the referendum was in my opinion masterminded to create the atmosphere in which it was possible to get agreement to a pay policy and drop the industrial policy. Thereafter the Social Contract completely evaporated. I don't believe we could have avoided that by saying, well, we'll just stay in Europe and leave it at that. The European question became centrally important in the development of the new industrial policy. The exchange control was weakened and so on, and all this was under Common Market pressure. Once the Treasury had the Common Market on its side, it was easier to dismantle the remains of the policy. It was a sort of mopping up operation. On issue after issue the Treasury or the foreign office would say, 'The Commission won't have this', so we dropped it; 'The Commission won't have that', so we dropped it. The issues of the EEC and industrial policy were very closely linked, and still are. If you don't break with the Treaty of Rome you are never going to be able to have an alternative economic strategy in Britain.

Did you make any attempt, either alone or with other colleagues on the left of the party, to lobby in the trade-union movement on behalf of the AES? It's often pointed out that Jack Jones and other trade-union leaders argued for guarantees on questions like pensions, but completely abandoned compulsory planning agreements or any sort of state intervention in the economy.

The morning after the referendum Jack Jones made a statement on television saying that the unions would not understand it if I was dismissed. That kind of sentiment evaporated within twenty-four hours, as you would expect. But the thing I found most painful was that there was really no top-level trade-union support for the industrial policy at that crucial moment when it was reversed.

Of course the referendum and industrial policy defeats did not end the battles. I campaigned with other colleagues for the alternative strategy throughout the period from early 1975 to May 1979. Around the time of Wilson's resignation I was actually able, as a candidate for the leadership, to spell out in speeches and interviews a complete alternative strategy and still remain within the cabinet (these speeches were published in a pamphlet called *The New Course for Labour*).

In the spring of '76, you'll remember, just after Callaghan became prime minister, there was a leak about proposed deferment of the child benefits scheme, which was saved as a result. I was told that a number of ministers including me were going to be interviewed by a chief inspector, in an effort to trace the leak. Since I had no knowledge of this, I declined to see a police officer, so I had a senior civil servant come and see me, and he said, 'We have three categories of suspects: those who believe in open government, those who keep diaries, and those who are politically motivated.' What are ministers supposed to be if not politicially motivated! Anyway, I said to him, 'I am at the top of every list, but I know nothing whatever about the leak' – which I didn't. That incident revealed – among other things – the intensity of the battles that were going on. We lost most of these, but not all. Several months later there was the battle against the July 1976 cuts – the ones intended to fend off the IMF – and then came the attempt, in October 1976, to cut benefits. In the course of this argument I circulated the minutes from the last days of MacDonald's cabinet in 1931 (these were available because of the thirty-year rule) which caused a great deal of anger. Those minutes were very useful, because they revealed that the cabinet of 1931 (of which my father was a member) broke on the issue of benefits. Although we lost on the AES, the proposal to cut benefits was killed. You could say that we were defending, with some success, a social wage against those who were trying to let that go down the chute along with the industrial policy.

From the Social Contract to the Cuts

How did the Social Contract originate, and how much hope did you yourself repose in it to begin with? After all, it did have a genuinely reforming edge to it initially.

It really concerned the relationship between the trade-union movement and the Labour Party. The divide was so deep after 1970 that for nearly two years the trade-union leaders actually would not meet the parliamentary leadership. It was around the time of my speech to the TUC conference, which you quoted earlier, that the TUC-Labour Party Liaison Committee was set up. But the early meetings of the Liaison Committee were frustrated by the fact that there was a school of opinion in the parliamentary committee and the shadow cabinet, of which Jenkins was a leading member and Prentice another, that was not prepared even to concede a commitment to repeal the Industrial Relations Act until they'd got something by way of return, namely an incomes policy. That caused a real tussle, and in the end it was agreed that the next Labour government would immediately and completely repeal the Act. That paved the way for the first statement we issued, on 28 February 1973, exactly a year before the election, a policy paper called 'Economic Policy and the Cost of Living'. The TUC was not prepared to agree to an incomes policy, beyond saying at the end that, on the basis of the policies canvassed in the statement, an incoming Labour government would discuss with the trade-union movement how to handle the situation. The unions couldn't go further, first of all because they simply were not prepared to, but secondly because the TUC can't offer an opposition more than it offers a government without undermining its position vis-à-vis the administration of the day.

Out of this joint statement came the Social Contract. It was not conceived as relating to pay – I remember drafting in one of the manifestoes the words 'the Social Contract is not solely nor even primarily about wages, but about a joint agreement to carry through economic, social and political changes'. *That* Social Contract – the one we needed – died with the virtual imposition of the pay policy in the summer of 1975 when, as I mentioned, the trade-union leaders really feared that without some support for the government, the labour movement's defeat in the referendum would be reproduced in a further election with a Labour Party defeat and the return of a Tory government.

But what was your view of the Social Contract that actually did come in summer 1975?

I was very doubtful about it. During the referendum a very senior civil servant with whom I was discussing the matter somehow indicated to me that as soon as the poll was out of the way they would begin work on the pay policy. By then, the party in my view having been defeated, the right-wing had their own terms for a settlement, and these included a pay policy. There was considerable resistance to this, and a bill to make it statutory was in preparation. I was involved with others (I was by no means the leading figure), in resisting such a measure. Of course throughout the period 1975 – 78, the position of those in the cabinet who were doubtful about, or opposed to, a pay policy was very much weakened by the assent that was forthcoming from the trade unions themselves. This came out at the Tribune meeting during the 1975 Labour conference, when Ian Mikardo made his speech implying that the union leaders had given too much for too little. Jack Jones was so annoyed that he got on the platform to protest. In the autumn of 1978, when the TUC and the Labour Party had rejected the pay policy, I put in a paper to the cabinet – it was the only paper I put in on the subject – saying that we should not stick to the 5% limit. Callaghan refused to circulate it. You see, this was not a battle that a left minister could fight in the cabinet when messages were continually coming in to the effect that there was a degree of consent to the policy, indeed more than a degree of consent, in the unions. The miners actually had pithead ballots on it – and the coal industry was then part of my responsibility. You couldn't outdo the view that was being accepted at that time by the unions themselves.

Comparing the July measures of 1966 with the October cuts a decade later — presumably the battle lines between right and left were much more clearly drawn, notwithstanding the role of someone like Crosland. . . .

It's as I described earlier: at critical moments the issue was always presented as a question of confidence in the prime minister. And Callaghan played it extremely cleverly. There were various ways the cabinet could have discussed it. One was to say: 'Are we prepared to accept the IMF conditions or not? If not, what shall we do?' But instead the prime minister decided that the first item would be the alternative strategy, so I was put on and spent a whole morning having my paper torn to shreds. Once the alternative strategy had been defeated, the question was, what was the best deal we could get from the IMF – who were without any doubt being encouraged by domestic influences – the City and the Treasury. When the IMF conditions were put as a confidence issue, Crosland said: 'It's mad, but we have not got an alternative'. That was the moment when social-democratic revisionism died in the Labour Party. It was killed, not by the left but by the bankers. Crosland knew it was absurd to return to stop-go and cut public expenditure, but he conceded on grounds of loyalty to the prime minister.

Were you very isolated at this particular moment?

We kept lists of the cabinet line-up – the cutters, the supporters of the alternative and the wobblies. We hoped and believed that the wobblies, once they realized the price of cutting, would come over to us; we misled ourselves into believing that if it came to the choice between a Tory and a socialist policy, the social democrats would come with us. They didn't of course, and I should have known they wouldn't. So we were very heavily defeated – a minority of six or seven, no more.

The conclusion you drew from the episode, then, was that this was a third round of revisionist reduction of what the Labour Party had come to represent: first the attempt to strike away Clause Four; then the move against trade unions; and now the abandonment of full employment and minimum welfare provision. Even though it also meant defeat for one of the main revisionists, namely Crosland?

When Crosland said of local government expenditure, 'the party's over', he was really beginning to chip away at his own alternative to socialism. The great theme of *The Future of Socialism* was, you don't need socialism because capitalism is now working and we will always have full employment and the welfare state, and public expenditure will redistribute the wealth more humanely than Tory ministers will. When that perspective was abandoned – Jenkins led the way, saying that political liberty is at risk if public expenditure rises above 50% – their party really *was* over.

The Right and the Left

In a way the social democrats must have found the experience of the Callaghan government as deeply disenchanting as you did, even though many of the decisions may have been going in the direction they wanted. Didn't they still feel that the government was being continuously impeded by an institutional trade-union pressure? Perhaps this would explain why they broke with the Labour Party only two years after that government fell.

Well, I think the right wanted to split the party from very early days. In 1960 Tony Crosland wrote to me and made that clear. He said the same to Gaitskell. That was twenty-two years ago. Gaitskell without a doubt wanted to shed the socialist commitment in Clause Four, though he did not want to break the trade-union link in so far as the trade-union leaders were the praetorian guard then protecting the parliamentary leadership from the constituencies. But there has always been a desire on the right to split the party; their argument has been about *where* it should split. They wanted the left to leave and wither on the bough, as the ILP did. In the end that failed and the SDP was formed. The Social Democrats left the party because they had failed. The Labour Party is too strong, too deeply rooted in the trade unions and in socialism and too self-confident ever to be taken too far away from its real purpose of transforming society. The right – or some of them – became pessimistic, and they left when they realized that if they could not achieve their purpose in the government, in opposition they were absolutely finished.

There is a danger of a sort of cant in saying that the Labour Party can't ever be taken too far away from its original purposes. The problem is the opposite. If its objectives are those proclaimed in Clause Four, the main difficulty seems to lie in getting it anywhere near them. Wasn't there something, in this period specifically, that traumatized the proto-SDP? Earlier on you referred to Wilson's pessimism about the miners strike and its consequences. Was it not the tremendous working-class upsurge of 1973–74, and the perceived political power of the unions thereafter, that triggered off the eventual split?

Yes, I agree with that. The election of Wilson as leader in 1963 had worried the right, because they had supported Brown or Callaghan. Then *In Place of Strife* failed, as the attack on Clause Four had failed before it. Then in 1973 – 74 there was this industrial militancy and an extraordinary socialist upsurge, and they lost control of policy-making on the national executive. Crosland tried to retrieve the position but he couldn't because there was such a head of steam behind the movement. The three-day week was the climax of this. Then came the March 1974 election: the cabinet majority were saddled with a victory they had not expected and a policy they did not believe in. The Establishment did believe it, however. There is no doubt that in March 1974 the British Establishment was more frightened than it had ever been since the General Strike. We could have done almost anything we wanted, even without an overall parliamentary majority. Wilson's great contribution was to restore the British Establishment's morale by dropping party policy, and by the summer of 1975 the party was in retreat.

The social democrats won the referendum, and thought they were home and dry. They then had a string of remarkable successes culminating in the decision to go to the IMF. But that was a bittersweet moment, because the price was more than the social democrats wanted to pay – the obituaries to Crosland were in effect obituaries to social democracy. The Lib-Lab pact gave them a new lease of life, a new way of fending off the left. But then came the 'winter of discontent' and they realized they were up against something too strong. I don't mean by this that pure socialism was dominant in the Labour Party, but the party as representative of the working-class interest *is* too strong to be shifted far off course.

Yet you've made it plain that your own experience, the experience of the left, was if anything more frustrating. How would you summarize the 1974–79 administration compared with that of the 1960s, from your point of view?

Well, it was a re-run in many ways, allowing for changes and the fact that the situation was more difficult, the options narrower, and so on. The difference from my own point of view was that the preliminary radicalization at the end of the sixties had developed and become pretty fully formulated during the period in opposition. I was secretly afraid, returning to office in 1974, that the pressures of government would lead me to abandon the views I had then reached, but I found that they did not; indeed quite the reverse, they strengthened them. I was therefore much more courageous in cabinet, and argued what I thought quite freely throughout. On the other hand, the defeats suffered in the 1974 – 79 period were much more serious ones, because as I say the choices had narrowed as a result of the deepening crisis. The screw was tightened, with the cuts in public expenditure and the rise in unemployment. It was increasingly difficult, in cabinet, to get the words 'full employment' into our annual statement of economic policy, even as an aspiration. In some cases we had to fight to get them included. The EEC controversy created a very deep divide, but I must say that the Labour cabinet never succeeded in getting a majority of Labour MPs to support the Common Market. The left of the party was stronger at the time and the pent-up feeling was much greater, especially during the 'winter of discontent'. The determination of the party after 1979 never, never to go back to what had happened then, let alone what had happened earlier, became in the end a totally invincible force, and expressed itself in the TUC and at the party conference by majorities of about four to one. That was a fundamental change. The experience of the 1974 – 79 government has brought about an irreversible shift of opinion within the Labour movement, which no amount of press campaigning will be able to change.

In considering the factors that shaped my thinking over these years, I must mention the close political colleagues with whom all these events were discussed in depth throughout. No one person, especially if deeply involved in day-to-day decisions and public campaigning, can hope to draw the right conclusions or prepare plans for the future without the discipline, the analysis, the criticism and the encouragement of close and trusted friends.

I've been fortunate to have such friends and comrades,

and their contribution to the formulation of our shared view has been formidable. Some, like Michael Meacher and Bob Cryer, were ministers. Others, like Jo Richardson, Joan Maynard, Audrey Wise, Dennis Skinner and Stuart Holland, were colleagues in parliament or on the NEC. Then there were Frances Morrell, Francis Cripps, Tony Banks, Ken Coates and Chris Mullin, who were part of the campaign. Trade-union experience, especially among the shop stewards committees and the members of the general management committee of Bristol South-east Labour Party, played a very significant part. But Caroline was the principal colleague from the very beginning. Not only has she played a key role for twenty years in the development of a socialist educational policy; her powers of analysis, her understanding of socialism, her commitment to collective action made it possible for us to see our own way forward through the complexities and the confusion of the unfolding situation, and to survive the unrelenting media harrassment and misrepresentation.

Above all this, of course, nothing could have happened without a parallel development of opinion throughout the entire labour movement and beyond. This opinion has been formed from experience, and it has expressed itself in the unions, the constituency parties, the women's movement, among the ethnic minorities and in the peace movement. Those who share it can be found in the professions, in the civil service, in the media, and among radical groups everywhere. In thousands of private and public meetings I have attended, and in tens of thousands of letters sent to me, these experiences have been conveyed with criticisms, suggestions, and support. In this way, the ideas of democracy and socialism have reappeared on the national agenda and come together as an insistent demand for renewal. We are now at the beginning of a campaign to achieve that.

2
The British State
and Democracy

Your most constant distinction as a Labour politician, from the earliest days, has been your critical awareness of the state. Now — to begin with a general point — there seems to be a major contradiction in what you've said publicly about the British state in Arguments for Socialism *and* Arguments for Democracy. *In the former book, as you develop your case against the EEC, you say: 'The parliamentary democracy we have developed and established in Britain is based not upon the sovereignty of parliament, but upon the sovereignty of people who, by exercising their vote lend their sovereign powers to Members of Parliament to use on their behalf for the duration of a single parliament only. Powers that must be returned intact to the electorate to whom they belong to lend again to Members of Parliament they elect. . . .' The rights derived from this system 'have protected us in Britain from the worst abuses of power by government, safeguarded us against the excesses of bureaucracy, defended our basic liberties, offered us the prospect of peaceful change, reduced the risk of civil strife and bound us together by creating a national framework of consent for all the laws under which we are governed'. On the other hand, in* Arguments for Democracy, *we get a completely different general characterization of this same state, with the emphasis now on its extraordinarily undemocratic character. The opening essay says: 'Despite all that is said about British democracy, and our traditional free-doms, the people of Britain have much less control over their destiny than they are led to believe'. You argue not only that this control has actually diminished over recent decades, but also that the structure of the British constitution itself renders this a thoroughly undemocratic state. You mention the royal prerogative, the House of Lords, the patronage power of the prime minister, the nature of the courts, and so forth, and you conclude: 'The British constitution reserves all its ultimate safeguards for a non-elected elite. The democratic rights of the people can in crisis be adjudicated to be illegal'. How can you reconcile these two arguments?*

What I was saying in the first case – in December 1974, just before the referendum – was: be careful you don't give up the ultimate right to dismiss a government and elect another that will change the law and is then obliged to submit itself to your judgement, to be re-elected or defeated. The more I think about the democratic process, the more I see its impor-tance to be the capacity to remove a government as the ulti-mate popular safeguard. That is a capacity we have partially relinquished by entering the Common Market. The second case raises two points. First there is all that unfinished busi-ness left over from the constitutional settlement of 1688. Successive parliaments – and I have been a member of ten of them, over thirty years – have actually abandoned powers borrowed from the electorate to the executive, to NATO, to the IMF, to the multinationals, to the EEC Commission, to the security services, to the military, and so on. What I was trying to do here was draw attention to the *unfinished* busi-ness in developing democracy. The House of Commons has, in return for keeping up the status of members of parlia-ment, traded away its power to others to exercise, in ways that are becoming increasingly dangerous. The powers of the security services, which we are now told are not a legitimate matter for parliamentary discussion, are a vivid case in point. So I was saying: be clear that the issue is the sovereignty of the people – not recognized in law by the constitution, I might add – consider how far we are from realizing it; but don't forget that the ultimate power to remove governments is still there. When you try to use democracy you are going to find yourself crabbed and confined by all the concessions that have been made by successive generations of legislators, of which the most recent is most to blame. But I still believe that the power of dismissing governments is of fundamental importance, and one should never underestimate its potential for change if it is used properly, in conjunction with the labour movement, in the way that the Tories use the parliamentary arena in conjunction with their extra-parliamentary allies in business and finance.

But it actually has politically bad effects to embellish the nature of the British constitution, as you do in saying that sovereignty rests with the people, not with parliament. Technically it doesn't even rest with parliament but with the Crown-in-Parliament. . . .

That's the 'unfinished business of 1688' to which I was referring.

And socialists must insist that it is *unfinished. But there's a second point. This power to dismiss a government, important though it is, technically doesn't exist. A parliament elected in 1984 could perfectly well declare itself a twenty-year parliament, and there would be nothing illegal about that. In other words, the British constitution doesn't contain any intrinsic safeguards at all.*

The *intrinsic* safeguards in any democracy, however structured, lie in the attitudes of the people and in their willingness to organize to defend their rights. You can have the most perfect constitution in the world – the Soviet constitution is excellently drafted – but if it doesn't actually preserve freedom, if people do not insist on its having effect, it isn't real. Conversely, any attempt in Britain to prolong parliament would be such a breach of the *social contract* in Rousseau's sense that the moral legitimacy of the government would then disappear. If, for example, a government tried to legislate to remove the vote from women or from working people, or to give double votes to ratepayers, its moral authority would vanish. But even given the moral authority of democracy, there are of course a number of extra-democratic powers that prevent us from institutionalizing the sovereignty of the people – we in Britain are not even recognized in law as citizens; we are subjects. These are matters that three years ago might have been thought to be entirely for academic historians and lawyers to mull over, but this is no longer so. People are going to have to think about them more as the situation gets worse and the repressive measures introduced by the government intensify.

These safeguards that exist de facto in the democratic sentiments of the labour movement and other sectors of the population — shouldn't they be entrenched in constitutional provisions?

I agree with that. The only written constitution we have, strangely enough, is the Treaty of Rome. We still speak as if we were a country without a constitution. But we have one. The Treaty of Rome is our constitution, because everything is subordinated to it through the agency of the European Communities Act.

The Treaty of Rome is obviously a pernicious capitalist instrument — and we should return to the EEC later on. But Mitterrand, for example, hasn't yet found it an obstacle. The linkage you perceived, when you were in the department of industry, between resistance to the industrial policy and allegiance to the EEC's wishes, surely had less to do with Brussels than with the attitudes of the British state bureaucracy and the rest. So, in the end, the main problem is at home.

I do accept that many of the difficulties I had in implementing our policies were with Whitehall. But EEC membership greatly strengthens all those elements in our own state structure which are reactionary. In that sense, yes, you always come back to the nature of your own society.

1. Parliament and State

What then are the main items of this 'unfinished business' you've referred to, so far as the organization of the state and the legislature is concerned?

There are two broad headings. First, democratic advance was checked short of the point where it established a constitution in which the rights of the people were dominant and recognized as such. In the United States, for example, and in other democratic republics those rights have been recognized, in theory at least; but not in Britain. Second, measured in terms of real expenditure, there has been an enormous increase in the power of the state over the past sixty years. The functions of the state have proliferated correspondingly. The power of the state has grown in part through the reactivation of the old crown prerogatives, only now these are mainly exercised by ministers. A relatively minor example: the patronage of the prime minister has been exercised by use of the prerogative of creation of peers, which is outside parliamentary control. The prerogative of mercy too is of course still exercised in that way. More crucially, the security services are outside the democratic control of parliament. The old Army Annual Act, under which the discipline of the armed forces was subject to yearly renewal by act of parliament, was abandoned after the war, and security matters are virtually all determined by the use of the prerogative, not even by collective cabinet decision. The crown prerogative of treaty-making has never been subject to specific Commons ratification – and here I come to a very important point vis-à-vis Europe, namely that all law-making concerning the EEC is done under the treaty authorized by the European Communities Act, and so is not subject to specific legislation by House of Commons. The reason why the House of Commons never even discusses the EEC laws under which we are governed now is that they are arrived at by ministers exercising the prerogative powers vested theoretically in the Crown, which allow them to enter into agreements with foreign states. Our parliamentary democracy now finds itself with an elected monarch – the prime minister – who uses powers notionally vested in the Crown to bypass the legislature, which in turn has agreed to abandon key legislative powers. This constitutes a major reversal of the advances that we had made towards democracy, even allowing for the fact that we hadn't in any case completed the democratic process begun in the seventeenth century.

You suggested in the early sixties that the royal prerogatives be transferred to the Speaker.

Only two of them: the prerogative of dissolution and the prerogative of inviting a person to form a government. The Speaker is uniquely placed to know when a parliament has finished its effective life, because there is no prime minister with a majority, and similarly who is most likely to be able to form a new government commanding a majority. But I would not suggest that powers of patronage should be vested in the Speaker, nor the powers of treaty-making, or anything of that kind. Those are now exercised by ministers, and should be recaptured by the legislature as a whole. The only wholly discretionary prerogatives are those relating to dissolution and the formation of governments, and they are of course politically very important, as we saw in Australia when the governor-general dismissed Prime Minister Gough Whitlam and called a general election.

Monarch and Lords

Can we go on from the prerogative to the hereditary principle itself? You have been identified for a long time with the strug-

*gle for the outright abolition of the House of Lords, and it
seems that this may at last be incorporated in the party manifesto. But what about the hereditary principle in the supreme
symbol of the nation itself— the monarchy? One of the most
scandalized complaints made against left-wing tendencies in
the Labour Party is that they speak of the possibility of a
British republic, as if this were beyond the pale of civilized
political discussion altogether. Is it not necessary to raise this
as an issue in the labour movement — if only in an educational way, to begin with? Clearly the monarchy must have
important negative ideological effects, reinforcing social and
political hierarchy.*

The formal Labour Party position is that it assumes that the
Crown will behave constitutionally and therefore isn't an
issue. Republicanism has long existed in Britain. We had a
republic under Cromwell, and he abolished the House of
Lords, so there is a historical precedent for republicanism
which simply has to be accepted as a fact of our history.

As far as existing titles are concerned you can't stop people calling themselves what they like. But the abolition of
the Lords is and has been the policy of the party for a very
long time. The upper house has not been abolished as a
legislative body for a variety of reasons. First of all, because
of arguments about how to do it. But second, because the
real beneficiary of the House of Lords is the prime minister,
whose capacity to create peers is his greatest power of patronage; and many of the recipients of that patronage are in
the House of Commons. So you've got a common interest
between all prime ministers and some members of the
House of Commons and all members of the House of Lords
in their mutual survival, and that is an important consideration. As far as the Crown is concerned – with the exception
of the two personal prerogatives of dissolution and formation of governments, its historic powers are all now constitutionally constrained by long-accepted practices. If the
remaining prerogatives were vested in the Speaker, then you
would have in a pure and literal sense a constitutional
Crown, and that would reinforce the Labour Party's view

that a constitutional Crown does not raise a political question. But you cannot actually have a constitutional House of Lords in that sense, because the House of Lords has, and exists to have, legislative powers. (I leave aside the Law Lords, who have a different function which could easily be transferred elsewhere– say, to the judicial committee of the Privy Council.) However, whereas the Commons are the creation of the electorate, the Lords are the creation of the Crown. Therefore, if you are going to deal with the Lords, who certainly won't vote themselves out of existence, you've got to use the prerogative. You've got to swamp the House of Lords in order to abolish it. How can this be managed? Asquith went to George V in 1910 and said: 'We wish to swamp'. His reply was: 'I won't swamp without an election'. Well, if the Crown won't swamp without an election, then the best course is to begin by making 'swamping' an election issue from the start, on the very simple grounds that you expect if you win the election to have a majority in both houses, as the Tories always have when they win. Then, with majorities in the Commons and the Lords, you can abolish the Lords with public support. The way the Crown is approached is also very important. I have proposed that it be done by 'humble address'. The Commons would pass a humble address to the Crown – this takes the matter out of the secretive arena of a prime-ministerial audience at Buckingham Palace – praying that the Crown create enough peers to ensure a majority for our programme, which includes abolition. There are clear precedents here: when a Speaker retires, the House of Commons, by humble address, prays the Crown to make him a peer; and it was by humble address of the Canadian House of Commons in the 1930s that the Crown stopped making peers in Canada. So a whole range of instruments is actually available for dealing with the Lords. And if they cease to be Lords in law, or to have any legislative powers as such, and if the Crown is a constitutional monarchy in every particular without exceptions, then you really have reduced 'the hereditary principle' to the sort of heredity we all have, with mothers and fathers and grand-

fathers and grandmothers, and so on. You are then beginning to move to the completion of the unfinished business.
This is all speculative, of course, but we must be free to talk
about our constitution and these are proper questions to put.
This is the way I would see it, and if this were done, what
remained would have a certain familiarity to people and
need not inhibit the pleasures that derive from a long-
established tradition of some non-political kind.

*But even a constitutionally impotent monarchy would remain
an enormously potent symbol of inequality and hierarchy in
British society. Besides, one of the deepest cultural signifi-
cances of the Windsors is not that they embody a monarchy
but that they are a* royal family. *Their public status sanctifies
the institution of the family, with all its oppressions and inequalities.*

You've got to ask yourself whether the Crown simply
reflects inequality that is already there, or is the source of it.
A lot of the comment on the monarchy is cheap sniping
against the royal family as such, which is shallow and con-
temptible, and doesn't deal with the real problems we've
been discussing. If you look at the royal family simply as a
family, whatever you did constitutionally would not alter the
fact that here is a connection with a long history that will
remain in any circumstances. You can't pick out one family
who happen to be royal and say, 'They prop up the family'.
Nor can you say that the existence of families devalues or
threatens the existence of those who have different domestic
relationships, any more than I would argue that people living
in a gay relationship, or unmarried people with children, or
single-parent familes threaten other lifestyles.

*But the form of the royal family isn't merely one possible
domestic arrangement among other equally valid ones. It is
projected as a rigid standard — to which members of the royal
family must themselves conform. This is scarcely a private or*

*incidental matter. After all, the biggest constitutional crisis of
the monarchy in this century — the abdication crisis — came
about because the Baldwin government was determined that
the Crown should be seen to uphold a particular ideal standard of family relations.*

There is something in that. But if you are thinking as I am,
constitutionally and politicially, about how we can develop a
system that really does serve our democratic purposes,
there's a lot to be said for confining yourself to those aspects
of power, patronage and influence that we've been discussing here.

*So, then, Britain would be like India, republican in all but
name. . . .*

Many countries in the Commonwealth are republics recog-
nizing the Crown as head of the Commonwealth. The Lords
is a separate question. What I find so interesting is that
people say, if you abolish the Lords you threaten the monarchy, when they are really saying, let's use the monarchy to
keep the Lords. That argument brings the monarchy into the
centre of political debate.

*Why couldn't the House of Commons with a Labour majority
just pass an Abolition of the House of Lords Bill twice and be
done with it?*

Because you can't, I understand, carry through the abolition
of the Lords under the Parliament Act. There is some barrier to it. I understand that this Act, which provides for a
period of delay, does not apply to two things: the extension
of the life of a parliament, or the complete abolition of the
Lords.

Couldn't you just pass an Act rescinding this?

No, because, at present, you'd have to get the Lords to
rescind it! I should add that there is actually a sound con-

stitutional basis for believing that you have to abolish by prerogative. The only answer is to swamp the Lords with enough peers to pass the Bill. The Lords would have to accept this.

The Privy Council

You are yourself a member of another potentially very powerful constitutional relic, the Privy Council. Didn't you once suggest it as the substitute for the House of Lords?

Yes I made the suggestion in a pamplet I published in 1957 before I had woken up to the dangers of patronage. The Privy Council is in practice a purely formal body. It is called together only to announce the death of one sovereign and to declare the accession of the new one. I have never been to a full Privy Council meeting, because the last one was when the queen came to the throne. The cabinet is a committee of the Privy Council, and in that context it's part of the basis on which prime ministers exercise prerogative powers. This residual power where 'Her Majesty may, by Order in Council. . .', rule a certain thing, is a prerogative external to the Commons. For example, university charters are done by Her Majesty in council. This provision governs all sorts of interesting constitutional items that have never been fully explored: the status of the Channel Islands and the status of the Isle of Man depend upon order by Her Majesty in Council. But all that said, the Privy Council is not too significant; it's just another example of the need to place prerogatives at the disposal of the Commons.

Judge and Jury

The Denning judgement on the GLC's cheap transport policy is one of several that shows the decisive reactionary potential of these apparently antique constitutional provisions. Doesn't the whole constitution of the judiciary need the most drastic democratic overhaul?

Yes, but you have to be careful not to say that any incoming government can interpret the law as it wishes, without actually changing the law. The last Labour government was caught on the Industrial Relations Act, which continued to be implemented until we were able to repeal it. This is very frustrating, but I wouldn't want to get into a position where, for example, without going through the process of legislation the prime minister could simply tell the judges what they were to do. I wouldn't favour our trying it either, however convenient it appeared. The problem about Lord Denning is a rather different one. His judgements were bad and politically biased – I believe that very strongly. But the real danger was more general. Look at his Dimbleby lecture, where he argued that the British judiciary should be able to rule as contrary to the public interest any laws passed by parliament. Now that was a most staggering claim – a fantastic claim to power of a mediaeval character – and it has done great damage to the reputation of the judiciary.

The whole make-up of the judiciary represents a blatant form of class justice. Democratic reform of legal processes is essential, surely, with all due respect to considerations of judicial independence.

There are all sorts of problems about the legal system. As a member of parliament who has dealt with thirty or forty thousand individual cases, I don't think I have ever recommended anybody to go to the courts. It is expensive and you are not sure what the outcome will be. The very fact that the law is seen as being beyond the reach of the majority makes the case for law centres, and for a national legal service. The problem of the top judiciary is again one of patronage. It could be argued that judges should be elected, or appointed subject to parliamentary confirmation, rather as in the United States. That would be a safeguard. The age of retirement from the bench should be fixed. Again, a lot of the laws that the judges administer now were passed by parliament before there was universal suffrage, so the question arises whether laws should not automatically expire after a certain time, unless parliament reconsiders and reaffirms them.

Shouldn't the jury principle be extended right the way up, so that while expert legal advice would be available, at the end of the day ordinary citizens would interpret the legislation and make the necessary decisions?

The Law Lords, or the House of Lords sitting in a judicial capacity, really deal with matters of law. Juries determine matters of *fact*. They are guided on the law by the judge, who specifies the questions they must answer, and when they've determined the fact – guilty or innocent – then the judge applies the law. The case of civil legislation is rather different, of course, but I don't know that one could simplify it in the way you suggest. Where the jury system does apply, of course, if by that you mean a lay system, is in parliament; the House of Commons is made up of lay people who actually pass the laws.

The Armed Forces, Security and Secrecy

Again you come back to the idea of parliamentary control. How would this bear on the armed forces and the security services? The home secretary and the ministers of the armed forces exercise the relevant prerogatives in a rather notional sense. In fact the queen and the various members of the royal family all enjoy posts of military command. One has the impression that officers of the British army, when they swear a loyalty oath to the monarch, believe that this is literally what they are doing. They do not believe they are swearing an oath of loyalty to parliament.

It is important to be aware that we have 'Her Majesty's Judges', 'Her Majesty's Government', 'Her Majesty's Armed Forces' – that is what happens in a constitutional monarchy. But you have to distinguish the case where the secretary of state for defence, in conjunction with the prime minister, has by long convention the practice of giving advice which is accepted by the Crown, from those circumstances where there is uniquely reserved discretion.

Do you think that Michael Foot could appoint you minister of defence and that you would therefore have real command of the British armed forces?

Constitutionally, the armed forces are answerable to the Crown. But ministers are supposed to be in charge, under the prime minister, who can appoint whom he or she likes.

These constitutional instruments defend oligarchical power within the armed forces, and this in combination with the technological conditions of modern military organization and practice create an extraordinary state structure quite sealed against democratic control. . .

Here I come back to the old Army Annual Act. That provided real parliamentary power over the armed forces. If you were to take the situation where the armed forces refused to obey a minister, and you still had the Army Annual Act, the legal power to discipline the army and use it against the elected government would disappear on the day the Act expired each year. This was a very important safeguard, and we've lost it.

Do you think there should be an extension of democratic rights for soldiers and other members of the forces, and if so what type of rights?

I am strongly in favour of trade unions in the armed forces. These already exist in West Germany, Sweden and Holland. And what we're talking about here is not simply the right of individuals to join a union as part of their transition back to civilian life; it concerns the rights of soldiers collectively to discuss and negotiate over their conditions of work. I also think the Police Federation should be organized like an ordinary union.

Can we discuss the security services now?

Matters here are getting progressively worse. For example, guidelines were recently published by William Whitelaw showing that in 1977 the power to intercept telephone calls had actually been handed over to chief constables, although until quite recently it was always protested that each one was the subject of an individual authorization by the home secretary. I take a very clear parliamentary line on this. I believe now in returning to the Army Annual Act, which would cover the security services as well. That would be a minimum, but it would be a very powerful instrument, rooted well back in precedent.

Your proposals for measures to begin to control the security services are very welcome, as is the essentially related proposal for a comprehensive Freedom of Information Act. But what is the attitude of the dominant Labour leadership to these issues? The inertia and apparent indifference — or perhaps outright hostility — on their part is quite extraordinary. Why is it that measures like this seem to run into such stubborn obstacles inside what should be the major democratic movement in the country?

That's a very interesting question, because we were committed to a Freedom of Information Act in the 1973 Programme for Britain. After the 1974 election the initiative was handed over to the Home Office, who produced a first draft White Paper – and I think a public statement – in which it turned out that the civil servants' reaction was to say: we will reform the Official Secrets Act, because it is too weak. Far from enlarging freedom their intention was in fact to narrow it. Well, that was so unfavourably received that it came back to the cabinet. At that stage it was recognized that there had to be some real change, and I was put on the committee concerned (I had been kept off it at the earlier stage). Then Clement Freud introduced his bill and it turned out that an overwhelming majority in the House of Commons wanted real freedom of information. That produced absolute panic, and there were urgent meetings of ministers trying to hold the line against a House of Commons that was bending over backwards to implement Labour policy!

This episode revealed many things, in the first place the deep hostility felt by many ministers towards a Freedom of Information Act. But second, it blew a hole in the argument that we couldn't implement our programme because we didn't have a majority: the majority was there for that even if not for other things. In effect, the episode opened up a divide that should have been opened up long ago, between the executive and the legislature. Don't think I am in favour of an all-party approach to everything, but in this case there was a genuine legislative conflict with the executive. There was more hostility to the idea of a Freedom of Information Act than to almost any other measure, because it really touched the centre of power. Knowledge is power, and weak ministers and strong civil servants – we have had plenty of both in British government in recent years – live on the maintenance of secrecy: they can't be challenged.

What is the position today?

Well, it should be in the manifesto and there will be another great struggle about it. . .

What about reform of the security services?

My proposal in 1978 that the NEC hold an inquiry into the security services was very unpopular with Labour ministers, and I don't think any facilities were made available to the study group. But it is completing its work now, and I believe it will come out with a very strong report. On that issue there is going to be another huge tussle between the labour movement and the next Labour government.

How can we be sure that the measures will fare any better next time?

They will be very strongly resisted. The struggle would pass through two stages. First, the rank and file of the party must get the leadership to adopt the measures. The party, together with the House of Commons, which has a vested interest in controlling the executive, and public opinion, which supports this, will have to force its view upon a reluctant cabinet. Then, the cabinet, if it is persuaded or forced to proceed, will have to impose its will on the security services. That will be a very long-drawn-out battle, but it has to be won if we are going to make real my claims that the people are sovereign and parliament is their voice.

2. Parliament and People

Referenda and Popular Initiative

You've talked about the relationship between parliament and the various institutions of the state. Let's turn now to the really fundamental political relationship — that between, as you have just put it, the sovereign people and their parliamentary 'voice'. In your Llandudno speech you said that a five-yearly cross on the ballot paper is not enough, and argued that the referendum should have a place in the British political system. In fact, you pioneered the first ever referendum in Britain, over the EEC. You've explained how cynically this device was used on that occasion, and the devolution episode has given us further evidence on that score. But would you like to see it regularized as an institution in Britain?

In principle, yes, but there are problems. First let me say that what you would call the parliamentarian's dislike of the referendum, based on the belief that parliamentarians are more civilized and mature than the public as a whole, I do not share or accept. If you believe in the ballot box as the ultimate discipline of society or of government then you cannot really say also that it's got to be limited very strictly because when it comes to the actual administration of society or the development of the law there is something specially qualified about the parliamentarian. Nor do I believe that it is only the representative nature of government that protects us from a savage populace. This is the current view, and it has even been carried to the point where some people have said that the House of Lords, because it isn't elected, is able to be more enlightened on certain matters. I don't accept that. Take one example, the common one of hanging. It is said that it is only because parliament controls these matters that we are not a nation of hangers. My own opinion is different. The reason the House of Commons, over many years, has always voted freely for the abolition of hanging is not that the quality of members is higher than the quality of the people they represent, but that MPs were responsible for every hanging, and the knowledge that people were being hanged imposed upon them such a sense of responsibility that in the end they rejected it. So whatever attitude you adopt towards the referendum you should not argue that it is wrong because MPs are more civilized. Once you say that the people you govern are fundamentally untrustworthy except for the purpose of voting every five years, you have actually blown up the whole democratic case.

Now, let me take a look at the referendum issue from a practical point of view. I have already argued that the real strength of our present democratic system, often misunderstood, lies in its destructive power, its capacity to remove governments. Anything that weakened that capacity would be putting an axe to the root of the tree of accountability. It is the knowledge that every member, or every government, may be defeated that forces MPs and governments to listen to the public; when they face the public they are responsible for what they have done. There are certain things you could do to lift that responsibility from them, and one would be a referendum. Having advocated a referendum on the Common Market – which was right – I found myself at the end of the 1979 parliament as a candidate in my own constituency, and people said to me, 'Why have food prices risen under the Labour government?' I was able to say, truthfully, 'Well, you voted for the Common Market, I didn't. I was against it. I recommended you reject it.' The people had taken the responsibility for voting 'yes' to the EEC. The referendum had muddied the waters and made the allocation of responsibility more difficult.

Another factor that has influenced me is that a referendum where you are talking about an issue without personalities – a very pure type of democratic exercise – hinges critically upon the role of the media. In summer 1975, when every single newspaper apart from the *Morning Star* was in favour of our remaining in the Common Market, and the BBC should have been independent, but like ITN, was not, you had a situation where eight million people were totally unrepresented in the crucial public debate. There is no doubt whatever that had there been a referendum before we went in, with fair media coverage, the mechanism would have worked much more fairly. We have to be very careful with that argument – for we are not saying that the media is so unfair that we can't even have general elections. But it is a fact that on that occasion the public was denied access to the full range of information needed to reach a judgement – was conned, in my opinion into believing that the situation was going to be better than in the event it turned out to be.

Those are my two qualifications, then. I would not rule out the possibility that the referendum mechanism may be desirable, but it would have to be carefully structured so that it was deployed by popular initiative, not a plebiscite organized by the government on a question of its choosing, because that could be set up in such a way as to furnish constant confirmation of government policy. You could have a big press campaign against the trade unions, then have a referendum to make trade unions illegal. There is something about the right of popular initiative in Switzerland that I've always found interesting. The idea that people could have the right to convert matters of controversy into formal democratic occasions is a good one. Nuclear disarmament, for example, could be 'converted' into a referendum in which people would have to have the right to reach a judgement. That has potential, but you've got to handle it very carefully because the constitutional system is very delicate; people don't always entirely understand where its strengths and weaknesses lie, and you could have a clumsy surgeon accidentally cutting the central nervous system in the attempt to make it more democratic.

Surely one simple way of entrenching a provision for referenda is to say, as the Irish constitution does, that any matter pertaining to the constitution must be determined by referendum. That's not so delicate, or even radical, an operation.

That was the reason why I advocated a referendum on the Common Market. The same argument was taken up in the referendum on devolution in Scotland and Wales. But having said this, I think I would qualify it in this way. First, I no longer regard a referendum as being binding for all time. I believe that what happened then was just like an election. You accept the outcome of a general election, but you then go back and fight again; and since the Common Market proved such a disaster, there's nothing wrong about saying that we'll go forward and try and get it changed again. Second, it's argued now, by some, that since we voted to stay in the Common Market by referendum, the next Labour Government ought again to make EEC membership a separate issue and not tie it up with a general election. The practical position on that is that all our economic and industrial policies involve a massive intervention in market forces, which is illegal under the Treaty of Rome. If we go into the next election and say, 'Vote Labour and we will do all these things, but we will put the question of Common Market membership to you separately in a referendum', those who vote to remain will then actually be cancelling the result of the election they've just had. We would be misleading them. The next time around we've got to put the whole package of measures *and* the associated constitutional changes necessary to give effect to them. Otherwise we will be offering options that don't exist.

The most fundamental question here is that of popular initiative. The Italian constitution, for example, provides for a vote to be organized on a specific issue if a given number of citizens so wish; and this has been used to very good effect on the divorce issue, where a long overdue democratic reform which all the big parties were completely against was forced through. This resource has been used with negative results in some American states, but it will probably be positively used over the Nuclear Freeze proposal. Surely something along these lines, based on popular initiative, would be a positive supplement to any form of representative government.

I think that's true. I daresay if you look back at the origins of it, and I never have done, that the petition to the House of Commons was really a primitive and now stunted and decayed form of popular initiative. There's a petition bag behind the Speaker's chair, and people would turn up and present petitions. I think that the last time a petition was presented on a big scale was in about 1948, when the Lord Mayor and Aldermen of the City of London turned up in person and petitioned parliament against the abolition of the City as a separate constituency.

The second point I would make is that there is an alternative to referenda, namely a shorter parliament. I have always felt that the Chartists' demand for annual parliaments had got a lot more going for it than we've ever recognized. I'm not arguing now for annual parliaments, but if we did have these instead of two or three referenda a year, people would have a more regular vote, and they would be voting on the package rather than on individual items, often artificially separated, which is very important. I favour the four-year parliament as a possible alternative. But the role of the referendum is an area well worth further discussion; it has not been properly explored.

You are basically arguing that the only effective and responsible democracy is one with a representative element; but that is not necessarily the case. You have got to have structures of representation, but what is wrong with ordinary citizens being able to assume responsibility for themselves, periodically casting their votes on a determinate issue, rather than transferring that responsibility to one generalized representative body?

In principle that is a perfectly sensible proposition. One of the worst things about our present system is that public opinion is purportedly represented all the time through public opinion polls, which I believe to be one of the greatest contemporary examples of manipulation by those with the money to commission polls and set the questions, whereas government is by the representative system, and the apparent conflict between representative government on the one hand and public opinion polls on the other is that in the latter, the respondents are voting without responsibility: they know perfectly well that whatever they say, nothing is going to happen. When you link decisions with opinion polling, which is what the referendum does, you bring together the two ingredients that make true self-government and that is important. I might add that any popular decision, be it an election or a referendum, also compels a disclosure of information, because all sides have got to bring out all their arguments, knowing that the decision is going to be made by somebody in the street. So I'd go along with you on this point. But don't underestimate what I've said; it is important that governments be unambiguously responsible for what they do.

Do you think that technological developments might assist greater democratization? Interactive TV, or cable systems, for instance?

I used to think that. In 1968 when I was minister for technology, I talked about the technical potential of electronic referenda – and with multi-channel cable links in due course I suppose every home could be connected. I was laughed at then, and on balance I think it was really a mistake to think of it. First of all, the connection between voting, discussion and some form of action is very important; that's why I think the postal as against the workplace ballot leads to certain difficulties. I was trying to talk about people's capacity to influence events, not primarily about whether they could do this by pressing button B on their TV sets after they had seen a discussion on hanging. It is possible that in 50 or 100 years' time everybody will have a button. But even then the danger of manipulation through that type of voting would have to be taken very seriously.

But don't these technologies have a real and present potential as part of a system of workers control or self-management? Surely there is a strong case for the sort of system that was devised in Chile in 1972–3, whereby every enterprise would have a facility that could be plugged into the central economic planning computer and could inform itself about how its own decisions would affect or be affected by the national planning framework.

It is very helpful if you can call up a set of forecasts and then interrogate them. I spent a lot of time in the department of energy interrogating forecasts, and what I discovered in the end was what I should have guessed in the beginning: that all forecasts were based on certain assumptions, and these assumptions were all being fed in by somebody at the Treasury. Change the assumptions and the whole thing changed. So I don't think there is a mechanistic answer. Actually, the best way of introducing workers control would be to give workers the power to sack their management. I did once introduce a private members Bill to provide that under the Companies Act every company would have to satisfy the registrar of companies every year that their management enjoyed the consent of the workforce. That had great merit, because it introduced this 'destructive' element, this power to remove, into industrial democracy. Instead of voting on individual decisions which the management could simply reject as impracticable, workers could simply change the management, which would then have to listen to the work-force because the relationship would then be much more comparable to the MP-constituents relationship. People should have advisory services at their disposal to assist them in judging a range of options. But if the expert is moved into the centre of the democratic process, you put yourself in the hands of the programmers and the people whose assumptions are fed into the system to begin with.

Proportional Representation

All these reforms lie over the horizon of immediate politics in Britain. But there is one issue affecting the whole structure of British politics which is clearly going to be central in the next election campaign: the nature of the electoral system itself. The Labour Party is firmly opposed to any electoral reform, and you yourself have also spoken out against it. Why is this?

Well, it sounds cautious, but I'd begin by saying that in making a change in this area, you've got to be very careful of what the consequences are likely to be; second, you have to ask yourself, who favours a change and why? There are a lot of people on the left representing minority elements who favour a change, and they favour it for the obvious reason that our electoral system gives an added weight to big parties at the expense of small ones, so all new and small parties want a change. That is the practical reason why the Liberal Party, when it was in power between 1906 and 1916, was opposed to a change, and why in a later period, when the party had shrunk, it then came to favour change. The SDP, if it ever became a second party in Britain, would probably oppose proportional representation because their position might be undermined by it. I'm not even sure whether the Communist Party wouldn't adopt the position of all the major parties in such circumstances. Big business supports a change. The Hansard Society has been converted from a semi-independent organization studying parliamentary government into what seems to be a main agent in the campaign for PR. Why are they doing it? I think there are a number of motives. Without a doubt there is the belief, which I think is

broadly correct, that PR would lead to coalition governments, effectively paralysing the parliamentary process and
elected governments and leaving big business to get on with
their own affairs. How many governments have there been
in Italy since the war? And what resolution have they permitted of some of Italy's greatest problems? How often do
you see parliamentary paralysis opening the way to a military takeover, as in Turkey? So you have to be careful, before
you go into this as a purely theoretical exercise, to ask yourself just exactly who wants PR and why.

The second point I would make is an important one: in the
guise of transferring power from the politicians to the public,
PR really transfers power from the public to the politicians.
Under a system where a number of parties were more
equally positioned to seek public support – you would have
four or five or six manifestoes, you might have two or three
conservative parties, you'd certainly have two liberal parties,
and maybe two or three sections of the Labour Party free to
develop their arguments, and the electorate would appear to
have a much wider range from which to choose. But once the
ballot boxes were locked away the coalition government
itself would be assembled behind closed doors, and its
policies would never have received public approval at all.
That is the great weakness of coalitions. You think you have
a choice when you vote, but the final governmental outcome
will never have been endorsed by anyone. Also, by opening
up the possibility of endlessly reshuffling the governmental
combination, coalitions endanger the absolutely fundamental capacity of the electorate to remove governments completely. What has happened in the Labour Party since 1979
would never have come about if we had ended up still a
minority governing with Liberal suport. It has occurred only
because we were wholly rejected by the electorate. PR is a
marvellous way of *fixing* problems, but it is not a way of
solving them.

*You've skirted all principle here. Your position appears to be
purely pragmatic. OK, we have to be careful about who sup-*

ports PR, but how do you propose to answer the straightforward question, is it right that any party — it could be the Labour Party, at the next election, but it could be one of the other two parties as well — should get a large parliamentary majority with, say, 28% of the votes. Is this really the most democratic system we could devise? Second, your argument that the prevailing system produces stability is a highly conservative one. The most stable policy of all in this case would be what they have in the USA with only two parties and those not very different from each other. Is that what socialists should be defending? The third point can be made on your own ground. You say that PR is theoretically more democratic but actually leads to paralysis. Are you suggesting that Sweden, a manifestly more democratic society by any standards you could apply, with a far longer record of government by the equivalent of the Labour Party, has been paralysed by PR?

If you've got a good system, defending it is not a bad argument! The consequence of PR, as far as I can anticipate it would be to deny the electors true choice, dazzling them with a wide variety of options but actually shutting them out of the final decision. I think there is something much more honest, for example, about the Labour Party, which is a coalition, being forced to sort out its arguments before it goes to the electorate, which decides whether it is prepared to go along with that particular line of policy, rather than having three different manifestoes published, with the final decision taken after people have cast their vote. You might call that a pragmatic argument, but I don't think there is any great harm in it. Would I be satisfied to see Labour getting into power with 25% of the vote? No, of course I wouldn't. But if you are going to make really major changes, there is no alternative to winning enormous support, majority support, for what you want to do, and I see appalling dangers for this country if the system is so set that you have deadlocked parliaments over a long period, with real power being exercised elsewhere.

Why don't these arguments apply to a country like Sweden?

I don't know enough about Sweden to know how the system works or whether it has other disadvantages. What I do know is that there is a very important connection between a constituency and its member. Now under some systems of proportional representation, the party draws up the list and prospective representatives have to satisfy their party machine if they are to get anywhere near the list or high up on it. And if I were part of a multi-member constituency, I don't believe that people would be getting the same service they get from me as an individual member. Don't think that because people have a wider range of choices on polling day and because the representation in the House of Commons relates more closely, as it would, to the balance of political loyalties reflected in the votes in the country, therefore this would bring government close to or make it more account-able to the people. Now it may be that because of the nature of our society we wouldn't have coalitions all the time, but I tell you that the Lib-Lab pact was the worst period of gov-ernment we have had. It could not have been worse, because in the guise of being one sort of government we were actu-ally quite different. It was all done secretly; for example, Jim Callaghan issued instructions that no proposal was to be brought to the cabinet until it had been cleared with the Liberal spokesman concerned and the result was that what appeared in the House of Commons had all been quietly negotiated in advance.

The arguments against the present system are stronger than you allow, and in fact you have put some of them yourself. Even accepting the questionable assumption that a spate of coalitions means 'bad government', you have got to remember there is more than one kind of coalition. You can have coalitions of separate parties — which is mainly what you have been talking about — but there are also party coali-tions. Look at the USA, where you've got two large quasi-party coalitions, the maximum difference within each being

*greater than the 'average' difference between the two, and a
first-past-the-post system. Now there is a really entrenched
system of quasi-coalition government. Closer to home, you
yourself have just described the Labour Party as a coalition.
As things stand, can't an elector in Bristol say: 'I voted for
Tony Benn, who believes in this, this, and this; but see what I
got. . .'?*

The Bristol electors know what they voted for. If they were
just voting for my personal manifesto and then got something else, they could feel let down; but I always say, *this* is
what we have agreed on. I won't say they necessarily get it,
but what we are responsible for delivering to them is what
we agreed before we were elected. Now if you take the
American system, both parties are capitalist. But that is so
for a variety of reasons. The trade unions have long been
non-political, and the development of an alternative party
has never been taken on board. But as American capitalism
moves into its ageing process, I'd be very surprised if the
question of a workers party does not finally arise. Don't
attribute the character of American politics to the first-past-
the-post system. The real problem is that there is no fundamental political choice.

*Isn't there a danger for the Labour Party, if it maintains a
completely obdurate stance on this question? Actually there is
overwhelming support for some such reform right across the
board. If the Labour Party excludes itself from any consideration or public debate of a constructive sort about the electoral
system, the SDP and the media will have a clear field, and
what's likely to happen is that we will get the worst of all
possible reforms.*

No, the case for a change should be argued strictly on its
merits. I hope that the Labour Party will be the biggest party
in the next parliament. I hope and believe that in a couple of
years' time we will actually have an overall majority; but
suppose, for the sake of argument, that we are only the

largest party. The SDP would then hold the balance, and might offer us support in return for PR. There are two objections to this. If, having laboured so long to produce policies, we ended up in coalition that gave the Gang of Four far greater powers than they had in the last Labour cabinet, the effect would be totally demoralizing for the Labour Party. So what would be the alternative? My own opinion, for what it's worth, is that Labour should accept the invitation to form a government, and then go ahead with its programme on unemployment, Europe, the Lords, and so on, and if brought down would seek a general election. The public, seeing something really being done about the most pressing problems, would not favour a further election centred on the introduction of PR, which would be seen as a barrier to the continuation of Labour's programme, and you would have a 1966-type Labour victory. The SDP would be driven into its proper place,which is with the 'wets' of the Conservative Party. So it may take two elections to defeat the SDP. We may do it in one, but we certainly wouldn't do it by going to the public and saying, 'Vote for us and we will not only implement our manifesto but change the electoral system as well'. I don't think there'd be any support for that. PR would make Labour's policy virtually impossible.

The contingency we were envisaging, which is now quite widely discussed, is that the Labour Party could get a larger majority even than Attlee's in 1945 and still be the smallest of the three parties, in terms of the popular vote. What sort of political and moral position would it then find itself in? Do you think that it could just proceed with business as usual?

Well I think we would have to implement the programme upon which we were elected. The votes of only 16 million people kept us in the Common Market in June 1975, yet nobody queried that. Elections do two things: they do give power to a majority (which may indeed be imperfectly constructed because of the way in which the electoral system works) but they also build up a structure of consent among the defeated, and that is an essential ingredient in the success of a majority government. I do not believe that a Labour government with 400 seats would find it impossible to carry through its policy. But, of course, as it proceeded – and I hope its first act would be to deal with some of these fundamental power relationships – it must still try to carry people with it, because even elected governments do not have dictatorial powers, nor should they have.

The Role of Parliament

We've covered a very wide range of constitutional questions, including some really fundamental ones. Isn't it inadequate to tackle them piecemeal, as the Labour Party has done to date, if it tackles them at all? You're saying that Britain has a very obsolete and undemocratic constitution. Shouldn't this 'unfinished business' be taken whole, in a constitutional convention deliberating in the spirit of the Putney debates or the Chartists' labour parliament?

Theoretically yes. But, in practice, people's interest in constitutional matters derives from their experience. I would never have known as much as I do about the House of Lords if I had not had to spend ten years trying to get out of it; if I had just sat down and thought about it in a theoretical way I am not sure that I would have got very far or been very interested. But as it was, the constitution came to interest me very much, and I began to realize its relevance and its potential. If you are going to interest the public in these matters, you have to take them through this experience. For example, Londoners think about why they lost on the cheap fares case, then Lord Denning's Dimbleby lecture comes into focus, and so on. I am all in favour of a constitutional expert writing a book – and lots of books have been written about the perfect constitution from *Utopia* onwards – but I don't know that this would necessarily excite people. Take the Labour Party. Why did all these issues of party democracy come up? It was because Wilson vetoed the 25 companies, because 71 Labour MPs broke a three-line whip and took us into the Common Market, and out of that came the constitutional change in the Labour Party. It was dismissed as being arid nonsense, when actually it was highly practical; constitutions are practical matters. It may very well be that when the next Labour government tries to implement its policy, all these problems will come into focus, in which case it will be an advantage to have thought about them in advance. You've got to have a map of the territory that lies ahead, but it does not follow that you should have a sort of holiday excursion to territory you haven't yet reached, in the hope that people would like to go there. I am all in favour of the mapping work being done, but I think it may be a bit premature, until the relevance of that work becomes explicit, to invite the party to say in the manifesto, 'we'll set up a constitutional convention'. You have to proceed by experience.

Lying behind much of your argument and discussion there seems to be an idea that Labour could make a breakthrough to socialism via certain peculiarities of the British constitutional system and political tradition — via a sort of elected dictatorship indeed. There is something fundamentally parliamentarist in your whole approach: you think that parliament, enjoying together with the Crown a sort of nominal and absolute sovereignty (if we make exception of the Common Market treaty), is somehow a remarkable device that can be put to socialist purposes. You favour popular initiative, you favour workers control, you favour the jury system, you favour trade unions in the armed forces, you favour many democratic measures; but you keep coming back to parliament and see the fundamental transition taking place by virtue of its democratic sovereignty, rather than through developments from below — the development of different political instruments capable of imposing popular rule over the local ruling classes and the multinationals. . . .

I am *not* arguing for an elective dictatorship. I see the function of the parliamentary majority as being to unlock those barriers on the statute book that prevent these developments from below, and that's a wholly different concept. Maybe there are some people who do see it the way you do; but these nagging doubts that exist on the left about our way of doing it are in very marked contrast to the way in which the Tory party operates. Many Tories don't see themselves as permanent MPs at all. They come into parliament to do a job: they use the statute book to liberate the forces of capital that support them. I see our job, when we get there, as being to use the statute book to redress the balance in a way that allows this bubbling up of socialism from underneath to take place. I see a Labour House of Commons in this sense as the liberator unlocking the cells in which people live. If you do that, you find you have actually enabled the creation of socialism from below – not used the parliamentary majority to impose socialism from above. In either case, however, you've got to have a majority in parliament, because the present statute book is at the moment a major obstacle.

There are two opposed definitions of parliamentary democracy. One says: all that's happened from the arrival of William the Conqueror to the present is that the Crown has agreed to exercise its powers in conjunction with parliament. The other view is that by a series of massive extra-parliamentary pressures we have won a number of victories, including the right to dismiss our government totally – which is not something to be underestimated. My view is that while there is great democratic potential in these achievements, they remain under-utilized and incomplete. I regard the democratic agenda as the absolute priority. Actual management of the economy, important as that is, must be secondary to the capacity for full political industrial and social self-government, because without that you can't have the other.

3
Facing Britain's Crises

Northern Ireland

British democracy has long been marred, even by its own declared standards, within its own borders — in Northern Ireland. Would it be correct to say that for some twenty years after the war this issue was scarcely ever ventilated in the Labour Party?

The Government of Ireland Act, 1948, consolidated the existing position in Northern Ireland, and Attlee was quite ruthless in sacking a number of parliamentary private secretaries who had voted against it. But it wasn't really until the civil rights movement began that the issue went back on the agenda.

How exactly did Northern Ireland start to impinge on the Labour government of the day? Later on, of course, in the seventies, the next Labour government took over the administration of a kind of full-scale civil war in the North. Does this explain why, at this date, the issue is only partially starting to open up as a legitimate area of debate inside the labour movement as a whole?

Well if you go back to 1920, the Labour Party had a whole series of conferences on the question, and it came out very strongly against partition. I was brought up to believe that partition was a crime against the Irish people, and I think a lot of people felt that. During the Second World War, Ireland's neutrality was an issue of considerable concern to the British government. But by the end of the forties Ireland really was off the agenda. The manifest oppression of Northern Catholics by a succession of Unionist governments eventually sparked off the civil rights movement, and I must confess I didn't think about it very much until 1969, when the cabinet decided after a lot of heart-searching to send the troops in. The 1974–79 cabinet didn't really discuss Irish policy at all, apart from the Ulster workers strike, which broke power-sharing in May 1974, and one or two individual issues. Bipartisanship hung like a pall over both parties. I recall writing to the prime minister – I think around the end of 1978 – to ask whether we couldn't have a debate in the cabinet and setting out some of the issues I thought should be discussed. That debate never actually took place, so we left office amidst warnings that nothing should be said in the manifesto that might lead to loss of life – this was the great fear, and the warnings were correspondingly effective.

It was only afterwards that the party set up the committee that produced the 1981 report restating our objective of Irish unity and committing us to abolish the Prevention of Terrorism Act. The trade unions played a very big role, partly because they had members there, and this became a factor of difficulty, because the unity of the trade-union movement in the North hinged very much on their not discussing the central question. But we did come up with something very much better than what we'd had. How we advance from there I'm not so sure, but at least we have broken with bipartisanship for the first time since the war, if not before.

In one crucial respect the Labour Party hasn't broken from bipartisanship, because it still supports the presence of British troops in Northern Ireland. You yourself have put forward an alternative proposal involving UN troops, but this position is desperately unpopular with the leadership, and it has not yet won a majority in a party conference.

Well, that is true. My proposal was not really a 'troops out now' proposal, because I think there is a certain over-simplification in supposing that if we simply withdrew the troops the problem would resolve itself. I don't think it would. However, the Protestant community in the North must realize that it cannot rely on British troops to back it up regardless of what it does to the Catholic minority; and I tried to turn my mind to the question of how you allay the fear that if British troops were withdrawn the whole situation would descend into an atavistic exchange of fighting and killing. Therefore I suggested that UN force might play a role. This undermined the basic argument for bipartisanship, which was that the military emergency was the dominant question and until that was ended there was no prospect of a political solution. The idea that the presence of British troops was part of the problem and not a part of the solution caused a great deal of official anger. On the other hand, the proposal won an enormous amount of public support, and having since explored the various types of peacekeeping force there have been, I do believe that the appropriate use of UN forces in the period of transition offers some relevant possibilities.

Isn't this really a more creative line of advance than the one that you've just commended, namely that of the Labour Party, which is after all a British party, in favour of a unitary state in Ireland? Shouldn't the final form of the state in the North of Ireland and the South of Ireland be wholly a matter for the communities who live there? Whether a new state is to be federated or unitary, or whether there is even the possbility of independence for all or part of Northern Ireland is really none of our business. Essentially it's not a British question but an Irish question.

I agree with that, but then I didn't say that the Labour Party would determine what type of structure there would be. The party would make it clear that it was not prepared to continue to accept responsibility for the handling of affairs in the North, and that if there were a security problem deriving from that decision, it would recommend as a member of the United Nations that this aspect of the transfer of power be overseen by that body. I've been very strongly opposed to those who say the British Labour party should organize in Northern Ireland, because that would constitute a reentry at the political level as we withdrew at the governmental level. But in Dublin, at a meeting not long ago, I did argue that the trade unions North and South, who do have a lot of links, should get together and begin to shape a Northern labour party linked in some way to the South. This would begin to discuss how to take over responsibilities that Britain could not and should not any longer discharge.

Still, you do have to think about how the vacuum will be filled after withdrawal. In that context, there are fraternal links that might at least legitimately entitle you to venture an opinion as to how it might be done. There has to be an element of consent in any system of government, and if the UN troops were to remain for forty years with no resolution of the problem, you'd be in an awful mess. But I don't believe that the work of developing an Irish solution to the problems of Ireland will begin until it is understood that British troops will not continue to be available for the purposes of maintaining law and order in the North.

There may be another Labour government in two years time, so this is not an issue that can be put on the back-burner. What could we realistically expect a Labour government to do?

That's very hard to anticipate. I think it would be very difficult for anyone to pull the manifesto back from the position adopted in 1981 – that a Labour government would work for British withdrawal and reunification; that while it would not concede veto powers to certain Unionist politicians, resolution of the problem would have to be based on good will. Whether one could inject into that – and I doubt it – the view that law-and-order aspects of the transformation would be seen as an international rather than a British responsibility is another matter. I think it's very doubtful whether we would get the right sort of commitment on that. But then it is also true that even Mrs Thatcher is trying to disengage from Northern Ireland; I think Paisley is right in supposing that there's much more in the Dublin-London talks than the participants will divulge. And I think that the Protestant community in the North realizes now that there is no will or desire in Britian to retain the status quo indefinitely by military force. The whole issue is beginning to shift into a new gear.

One interpretation of what you're saying is that we're now moving from one bipartisan consensus to another. That suggests that we could again have an election in which Ireland simply doesn't figure.

Oh no, I think there has been a major shift of opinion in Britain about Ireland. . . .

On which a new bipartisan 'discretion' could be based?

There are all sorts of quite major differences between the two main parties. Thatcher, in so far as she thinks about it in wider terms, considers the Common Market dimension – which is very different, and dangerous indeed. I've even heard it said that if there is to be a peacekeeping force, it should be a Common Market force. You're right: the statement we make on Ireland has got to be absolutely crystal clear. But I worldn't fear that it will end up in a new bipartisanship based upon nothing more than 'the Irish dimension'. That underestimates the extent to which the labour movement is really pressing for a change.

An undeclared war has been waged in Northern Ireland — a very complicated war, a civil war with elements of a colonial occupation as well. This has gone on now for thirteen years, without ever becoming a political issue between the parties in Britain. There's something very wrong with that.

I agree: there is a reluctance to discuss it. I would go so far as to say there is a reluctance to discuss any really important issue, not just Ireland. You can discuss the minor matters but the really big questions are too difficult, it is thought, and too divisive to be contained within the norms of political debate. But don't underestimate the importance of what the national executive recommended, and the extent to which the conference really wanted it – and probably wanted more if they could have got it. I cannot give you any undertaking that this policy change will go so far as to entail a timetable for a transfer of power, but there will be a change.

We've discussed the presence of the troops as a part of the large political equation. But there is a derivative issue, namely the actual activity of the British army in Northern Ireland. It's one thing to argue politically against 'troops out now'. But a question then arises — particularly sharply for a Labour government concerned with the state and its activities — and that is, what constitutes acceptable operational conduct in Northern Ireland? The record, under Conservative and Labour administrations alike, is appalling. This can't be discounted as an incidental expense, however positive the general political prospectus.

Yes, but are you talking about the conduct of an army in an internal security operation, or are you really saying that withdrawal now is the real solution? I've been rather reluctant to devote too much attention to this except in one respect, namely the way in which methods being perfected in Northern Ireland may be used at home. Are we going to find that the comprehensive low-level surveillance that has been part of the intelligence operation there is now going to be applied through the police in Britain? Leaving aside the possibility that you could resolve the problems in Northern Ireland by altering military orders or changing prison rules, there is no doubt that in this respect what's happening there is of immediate domestic relevance. Where you get levels of unemployment approaching those in Northern Ireland, you may get civil disturbance on a comparable scale, and you could find that the police and army trained in the Northern Ireland situation will quite naturally apply their new techniques at home. That is a very serious danger. On a number of occasions I raised queries about certain things that went on during the last Labour government – they were nothing to do with law and order, they concerned the civil-rights implications of nuclear power – and I was told, 'Well, we've done all that in Northern Ireland already'. So Northern Ireland became the benchmark by which to judge what could legitimately be done at home. In that respect what has happened in Northern Ireland is going to leave us with a legacy that we shall have to rid ourselves of by a much tougher policy of democratic accountability of the security services.

Devolution

The cohesion of the UK state is at issue in Scotland and Wales too. It seems strange that although devolution was not a particularly important issue for the labour movement as a whole in the sixties and much of the seventies, it was this that finally brought down the Callaghan government. The manifesto commitment to devolution was successfully obstructed both at ministerial and at backbench level, with decisive consequences for the government's support in parliament. What was your view of that whole process as it occurred? And where do you think this issue stands today?

You could indeed argue that it was devolution, together with the fact that one of the Irish MPs was unable to support us at the critical moment, that brought us down. But that would be confusing the occasion with the cause. The government had in fact come virtually to the end of its life by then. I was opposed to the Lib-Lab pact because I thought we would have done better to continue as a minority government proceeding as we thought necessary, and to say, 'Bring us down if you don't support us, and then we'll fight on'. The pact weakened us desperately during that period. It prolonged

our life uselessly, whereas what we needed was a prolonga-
tion such that the vitality of the government and the party
could develop again.

Devolution is still a live issue. However, at that time it got
bogged down by much too much constitution-making. There
was a special devolution department of the cabinet office,
and the whole issue became slightly rarefied. Second, it was
seen in isolation from very acute regional problems that
alienated a lot of people in the North-west and the North-
east. They felt that Scotland was receiving special treatment at
a time when there was acute unemployment in their regions,
so there was a backlash among some English members.
It would have been rather better, I think, if there had been a
kind of constitutional convention where people could formu-
late their demands. The government would then have considered to what extent it was possible to meet these. Perhaps
the process could have begun more slowly, say with a non-
elected assembly made up of local councillors, and
developed gradually from there. As it was, the devolution
plan was handed down on tablets of stone. It was taken out
of the arena of public discussion and put into a specialist
committee, and out of it came something that wasn't really
workable and didn't actually meet people's needs. We mis-
sed a very important opportunity there: if we had been able
to harness the excitement and enthusiasm of the people,
their desire to solve their own problems and to have the
freedom and the funding to do so, we might have turned the
tide. That would be my general approach. I wasn't directly
involved, as it happens, but I was strongly in favour of some
kind of devolution, as I have been for a long time. I feel very
strongly that as state power grows, it is getting more and
more difficult to relate the exercise of that power to the
perceived needs of the people in various parts of the country
with quite distinct conditions. For this reason devolution is
still on the agenda. I know the Scottish Nationalists' vote has
diminished, but I don't think the issue has gone away, and I
don't think it will, because we have a much too highly centralized system of government and we all suffer as a result.

Even in Wales your approach could have resulted in a much bigger vote for devolution. The real problem there seems to have been the fears in the non-Welsh-speaking parts of the nation of a sort of linguistic oppression. Had they been able to devise their own forms of local representation within a general devolution, the upshot would have been very different.

This question of approach has general validity, I think. (The Bullock report on industrial democracy was another case in point.) The way the Establishment responds to pressure is to channel it towards a special commission or committee, which then comes out with something so remote, so rarefied, so uninteresting, that nobody relates it to their experience; the original desire fades away and the Establishment breathes a sigh of relief. My own belief is that you should encourage much more discussion, for out of that will come something people actually want. But the Establishment is very cunning on these occasions. It's the old technique of the Royal Commission, really, although the Royal Commission itself was not used in this case. But there are other ways of achieving the same object, and we have seen some of them at work against democratic aspirations in England and Wales.

Economy and Society

There are forms of the AES that basically involve little more than a return to Keynesian reflationary policies with the addition of import controls. On the other hand, there are forms that begin to mount a real challenge to capitalist power, promoting workers committees and extending nationalization, and so on. But the most formidable single obstacle to implementation of a radical version of the AES would actually be the power of the City. How could a future Labour government avert the sabotage of its plans by the City and its allies in the Treasury and the international financial agencies?

You've raised two questions there. One concerns the meaning of the AES. Is it just reborn Keynesianism plus a little economic nationalism, or is it something more? Further clarification of the AES is an important part of what we have to do, although my own opinion is that events themselves will drive us to much more radical solutions. I take as a parallel my fifteen months at the department of industry: I had only Heath's 1972 Industry Act to operate with, but by injecting a little will into the implementation of that act, in the given conditions, it was possible to do an astonishing number of things. When you come to the City of London you're really talking about two things. One is the pension and insurance funds of major national institutions, and the question of harnessing their resources to the development programme. That will be dealt with in part by exchange controls, in part by the introduction of some democratic control of pension funds, which the trade-union movement has been pressing for over a long period, and in part it will be determined by the role of the banking system itself. It is interesting to recall that back in 1935 Labour was calling for the establishment of a joint-stock bank in a single, publicly controlled banking corporation; and I personally believe that the conference resolution passed several years ago about the public ownership of banking is an essential ingredient of a viable policy in this regard. I'm going beyond current party policy here, but I think we will really be driven to more radical solutions simply to make a full-employment policy work. I've long favoured our having a minister in charge of the Bank of England, with the governor under him or her. More recently I've been suggesting that the Bank of England, which is publicly owned, might be given powers of acquisition comparable to those originally devised for the National Enterprise Board. If you had a Bank of England conceived as a real public corporation with a minister in charge and having powers of extending the public sector, it would be possible to make a very sizeable impact upon the role of the City. If the £2,000 million spent by the Bank of England in 1974–75 in the lifeboat operation to save the secondary banking institutions had been available for the acquisition of those institutions, we could have moved quite quickly. In any case, some such moves will be absolutely necessary. The City would be quite ruthless in stopping a Labour government if it could. It would no doubt go along with us for a very short while, and then begin mobilizing with its supporters in the Treasury and elsewhere to put a brake on the new policy. In the end it will turn out to be a question of political will, a question of whether we're serious and really intend to carry out our plans.

So what kinds of commitments are going to be written into the AES before the election? Your argument seems to be that events themselves will push a Labour government in a radical direction. But all experience shows that 'events' tend always to drive Labour governments into accommodation. Without specific commitments and a party determined to enforce them, why should the next time be any less disappointing? Won't the Labour government once again be 'blown off course', in Michael Foot's phrase?

When I refer to the pressure of events I'm saying that once you *do* give a commitment to reduce unemployment to less than one million in the lifetime of the next parliament you are really setting yourself an objective entailing a great deal more than reflation and hoping for the best. Anything that fell short of a serious policy to that effect that would be noticed and rejected by the majority of the movement, and the public would lose faith in our capacity to do anything about it. Remember that between 1945 and 1947 the Labour government was driven by events in a way that was the very opposite of being 'blown off course'. I think we will be driven to do the same, but of course we should clarify the real problems at a much earlier stage.

But the strongest things that government did were put in the manifesto by Ian Mikardo, much to the displeasure of the leadership, insisting on putting a vote through the party conference. Who knows what Morrison might have settled for otherwise?

Yes, and that is exactly the point of the policy discussions that have been going on in 1982.

You said that the AES can't just be reborn Keynesianism plus economic nationalism. Well then, what further specific measures can we expect? In particular, what kinds of extension of public ownership do you envisage?

The case for public ownership, if it's presented simply on its own without relation to the objective you have in mind, has a slightly dogmatic and arid flavour. But if you say, let's be absolutely clear what we've taken on, and ask whether our commitment can conceivably be discharged while the multinationals and the City continue to exercise their present power, then the answer must be 'no', and against that background the case for public ownership reappears. You are right to say that the old and limited AES is simply not adequate. The IMF would be round within a matter of hours if you reflated on the scale that is now being contemplated; there would be an investment strike on a huge scale. Without a capacity to invest directly, which is what public ownership is all about, you would be at the mercy of the IMF and the multinational companies; and if you did invest directly and set up great state corporations then without industrial democracy you'd be back into dirigism of the old kind. These are the ingredients that must be added to the AES if it is to mean anything.

A successful move against the power of the City and a major extension of public ownership would be permissive conditions for tackling the objective of reducing unemployment to around one million. Wouldn't they also unlock the door, to use your own phrase, to the demands of the women's movement and the ecology movement as well as the labour movement itself for a full-employment economy where there were moves towards genuine equal work and pay for women and an ecologically responsible use of resources? And only with extensive public ownership could one envisage a generalized

*move to, say, a thirty-hour week. Shouldn't Labour, in for-
mulating its programme, bring these sorts of issues far more
prominently forward in its arguments for public ownership?*

Yes, though it would be wrong to try to create the impression that nationalization would usher in the thirty-hour week
and ecological responsibility just like that. The unfulfilled
function of the Labour Party and labour movement so far
has been in the clear statement and formulation of demands
quite openly raising expectations of what a Labour government will do and creating pressures that would be released
very rapidly once a Labour government was elected. When I
say 'events will move us' I don't just mean the pressure of
the City, but also the demands you mention – from the
community groups, from the women's movement, from the
ecology movement, from the black movement and so on.
The interaction of these demands with the policy commitments of a majority Labour government would really make
possible a major step forward from this basically unjust and
inequitable society towards something better. If we were
elected now, particularly after all that's been said about the
Labour Party by the media, people would expect a lot, an
awful lot more than they expected from Wilson or from
Callaghan, and unless the Labour Party has formulated
means by which these expectations could be realized there
will be deep disenchantment that will be very hard to
remedy. The pressure is on us now from a broad spectrum of
public opinion. It's a pressure that's been too slow coming;
people have asked for too little.

*You believe that an AES without any specific commitments to
the extension of public ownership would simply not be cred-
ible. . .*

Yes.

*But there is a second major issue — not completely absent
from the AES but not foregrounded either: workers control.*

Public ownership as an idea has been tarnished in England by the experience of the very bureaucratic Morrisonian corporation and all that went with it, plus incessant and prejudicial media attacks, but industrial democracy is something that nobody has any experience of as yet, and it is potentially a very popular issue. Even the Liberals and the Social Democrats have to pay some sort of lip service to it, though of course what they mean by it has nothing to do with progressive reform. What real institutional proposals can we expect from the Labour Party?

This is a very important question. A Labour Party – TUC committee report has just come out, because there is a recognition in the trade-union movement that change is essential. The Bullock report was not a success for a variety of reasons. One, it was taken out of the arena of public discussion into that of civil-service planning. Two, industrial democracy has to be seen as a further development of trade unionism, not a substitute for it, and the priority at the time was to reassert the right of collective bargaining and *then* to widen its scope beyond wages to prices, profits, personnel, planning, research and development, and so on. Another reason why trade unions have been a bit hesitant about industrial democracy is that they fear that if it rotated around the joint shop stewards committees it would interfere with internal trade-union structures. You also have to be careful that you don't unwittingly introduce a form of industrial democracy that entails breaking the link between local trade unions and the union structure as a whole. Some Tories would not mind pitchforking workers and their local trade-union representatives into a conflict with market forces: management would withdraw and the workers would be left to carry the can.

There are a lot of complexities here, but demands for industrial democracy will arise that will have to be met. However, it's going to be very hard to blueprint it in advance. Industrial democracy will express itself through municipal ownership, through the Greater London Enterprise Board and the West Midlands Enterprise Board, in what's emerging from Sheffield and elsewhere, and progress will be made, but I doubt whether any plan can be cut and dried before the next election. Almost by definition anything that is democratic has to emerge from discussions; it can't be handed down from the top and imposed whoever likes it or not. My experience has been that the type of industrial democracy people want varies very greatly according to their circumstances – the type of firm they work for, the relative strength of trade unionism, and so on – but whatever its forms, industrial democracy must advance rapidly if we're not going to end up with a more highly developed tripartite, semi-corporatist arrangement of the kind we've tended to have under the last couple of Labour governments.

What about the regular election of managers? That's perhaps the least immediate goal of a policy for industrial democracy, but without it there is no democracy at all, in the end.

I agree. If the people at the top could be fired by those at the bottom, they would learn to listen. Whether a proposal along these lines will be among our specific policy commitments I can't really say, but that would probably be the quickest way to popularize the idea.

One of the problems in this whole area is that there is often a tension between what the unions are willing to envisage or demand and what might be more popular with the mass of the workforce. The Bullock report did appear, among other things, to be enshrining the unions as virtually the sole representative of the workforce, whereas in reality the unions aren't simply a homogeneous institutional force. There are all kinds of conflicts and tensions between and within them, between the permanent officials and the shop stewards, between these and the ordinary members, on the other hand. How far can the unions be regarded as the shadow institutions of industrial democracy?

That sort of point is very easily misunderstood, but I know what you mean. The conclusion I have come to after many years' observation is that out of discussion where they work everybody will come up with something that best meets their needs. In the case of the Post Office, the union wanted to have workers on the board. I never throught very much of the idea, but we organized an inquiry and in the end they got what they wanted – so the UCW's rather old-fashioned Guild Socialist idea came to reality (though the present government has ended it). In another case, ICI set up what was basically a piece of window dressing. It became known as the Central Business Investment Committee, and was not based on the unions, but when this committee got going, rather like a mediaeval parliament it slowly began to acquire a cutting edge. A bankrupt company like IPD was prepared to try something entirely different, where all the power was in the workers' hands. So we have got to think in terms of *permissive* legislation where a whole range of workable options is provided for. People can then say, 'We want to move from status A, which is a private company under the Companies Act, to status B, where we have observers on the board or the right to dismiss our management' – and so on, moving by experience towards something that is real workers control. I don't think you can just work out from the top what is appropriate at once for the Steel Corporation, for Shell workers, and for the small business where what the workers want first of all is the right to be in trade unions. But provided we are clear and committed about the general objective and we have legislation of a permissive character and encourage discussion, we will have got all the ingredients of quite a big change. But the process is not like drawing up a new constitution: that way we'll end up with another devolution fiasco.

It may be risky to say so in one way, but we shouldn't simply identify the existing membership, structure and practice of the trade unions as the embodied interest of a homogeneous working class. For example wage-bargaining, free or not, is traditionally based on the family wage and on the assumption that the typical worker is a male bread-winner providing for a dependent wife and probably children. This has acted against the interest of women wage-workers and against the free entry of women into remunerated work. This case alone suggests that workplace democracy would not only have to take over all the inherited strengths of independently organized labour but would have to be framed in such a way that the inherited weaknesses and the simple prejudices of the trade unions as the dominant form of independently organized labour could be circumvented or checked.

There is a lot in the argument that if you build upon traditional trade unionism you carrying over the male domination associated with it, at any rate at the top level. On the other hand, in certain unions, for example NALGO, more than 50% of the members are women (one of the exciting things about the NALGO ballot this year was that the female majority could have determined the relationship of the union to the Labour Party). The nearer you get to the place of work the less the male-dominated union structure need operate, because there the balance of opinion will reflect the real balance of the sexes, and there are a lot of places where women are very strongly represented in the workforce. But I don't offer this as a remedy to the unequal relationship between men and women at work. There's got to be a great deal more pressure by women on the system if it is to meet their needs, and if that pressure is not forthcoming there will indeed be a reproduction of traditional male trade unionism at a new level. I would add to this the important point that collective bargaining as I interpret it covers something very much more than just wages, or the addition to wages. There's got to be collective bargaining about the chancellor's budget, about the distribution of money within the budget – as between, say, child benefit, investment and public services – and so on in every sphere. You've got to see the relationship between a Labour government and the labour movement as being itself one big and continuing process of open collective bargaining. Looked at in that way, the openings for the women's movement are much greater, if only the necessary pressure is there.

The idea that as one gets closer to the real place of work the balance evens out is a dubious one. Is it true even of the National Union of Teachers, with its large female majority and formal professional equality? The question of devising forms of collective organization with a real capacity to outstrip and to fight against the male-centred culture of the unions is a very important one.

I'm not saying that these would automatically develop, but that the scope for them to do so is greater. Old institutions reflect the values current at the time they were set up and new institutions will tend to reflect an altered perception of what is right. Clearly if you go into the home, which is the smallest workplace in the country, you may find male-female relationships at their most primitive, so I don't dispute that you've pointed to a problem. But the capacity to resolve it is greater if you open up genuine democracy lower down, and that is also true of democracy within the Labour Party.

You've spoken of many different and interesting ways of making possible more initiative from below. But you haven't mentioned what would have perhaps defined a socialist policy thirty or forty years ago: purposeful planning, an imposition of social priorities against a recalcitrant capitalist order. Surely a radical version of the AES will have to rediscover socialist planning.

That is already agreed. What's slightly worrying about it is that it's agreed to the point where planning could come to exclude all the things we've been talking about. But the argument for deliberate and conscious planning of our resources has already been won within the party and the unions and all these discussions about democracy are meaningless unless they are related to what in effect are planning decisions. You don't want power for its own sake, but to influence, and influencing at these levels *is* planning. The problem is going to be the interrelationship of all the local and sectoral demands with an overall plan. For example, if we go for major house-building programmes, the allocation of houses to different areas will be a very sensitive question, as the Yugoslav central government discovered in all its arguments with the republics. The conflict between national planning and local or workplace interests will be difficult to resolve, but planning as such is accepted.

Do you think that the existing institutions, whether of the labour movement or of capitalism, can provide the arena within which such problems are thrashed out, or do you think fundamentally new institutions will have to be created?

If there's an argument of a real and important kind going on, institutional arrangements for resolving it will tend to develop around the point of conflict. If for example, there is an argument about what resources should go to Scotland or to the North-east to deal with unemployment, that will breathe life into regional trade unionism, and so on. You've got to be very careful not to sketch out a perfect society in which everybody is fitted into a pattern willy-nilly. The working class must be able to initiate things rather than continue forever as a primarily responsive body. It must acquire a power of initiation that by law appears now to be confined to capital and to government. New institutions will develop in order to see that crucial decisions are not taken without regard to the interests of localities or, say, of women, because they simply won't have it and rightly not. But I doubt whether you can sketch them all in advance.

Let's turn briefly to several major questions of social policy, and first to education. If there is one reform that socialists will surely expect a future Labour government to carry out, it is the full and final comprehensivization of education. The creation of a real comprehensive system, with no exclusions, is long overdue.

I agreee with that entirely. The Labour Party has been in favour of comprehensive education since the twenties. What happened under the Labour government of 1945–51 is interesting, because when Ellen Wilkinson was education minister there were no real reforms towards comprehensive education. We are proud of the nationalization and welfare measure undertaken by the 1945 government, but as socialists we don't talk about its educational achievement, because so little was done. The role of the Fabian Society in maintaining consensual support for selective education against the National Association of Labour Teachers and the Labour Conference, which wanted comprehensivization, is only one aspect of an intriguing story. There followed a long line of Labour secretaries of state – not excepting Shirley Williams – who did not follow through and consolidate our policy for educational reform. Tony Crosland actually prided himself on the binary system in higher education (remember, we're talking about a fully comprehensive system, not just the secondary schools).

Labour's 1982 programme is a good one, though I concede that it has come very late. It takes a fresh look at aspects of policy that have been problematic. For example, the voluntary schools. Here we are trying to see how minority and ethnic groups can count on the public education system to meet their needs without adding to the number of voluntary schools. We also want to harmonize this sector more closely with county schools to prevent some religious schools being used to reintroduce selection by attainment, class or race in another guise. Fortunately, within the Catholic and the Anglican churches there is a strong comprehensive movement and a strong anti-racist commitment, and we can count on debate and support inside the Catholic and Anglican education communities.

The private sector is increasingly subsidized. By accepting such large subsidies it brings itself into our policy. We are restating Labour's longstanding objective of a non-feepaying, non-selective educational system. Local authorities would then estimate the community's needs and the facilities available to them, including private education, and would harness the facilities to the needs. If you can requisition the QE2 to take troops to the South Atlantic, why can't we requisition Eton to meet the needs of boarding-school education in the community? Why can't we requisition certain private schools to meet the need for nursery education? This, fairly presented, has the capacity to win great support, because a comprehensive movement, designed to meet community needs, is now widely supported. The Tories can't actually abolish comprehensive education, because parents don't want to return to the 11-plus. But they can and will attempt to erode it in every way they can. We must try to develop it.

For the 16-to-19-year-olds, it is important to develop the student trainee system for everyone, and gradually get away from the division at this age stemming from existing inequalities. The exploitation of youth by the Youth Opportunities Scheme should be superseded by proper education and training programmes, the expansion of post-18 education, including the Open University, and extended adult education. If we argue for all this properly, we will win great support. But our credibility in campaigning for this depends on our capacity to achieve full employment.

We assume that a priority for a Labour government would be the restoration and improvement of levels of social provision. But there is a great deal of justified popular discontent about the traditional forms of provision. For example, they often discriminate against households that are not nuclear families. And there is massive resentment about the dominant ethos of social provision — the air of petty tyranny surrounding so much of the dealings of the social services with their users. Although there has been some kind of commitment to the principle of provision, this has been honoured more often in the spirit of the poor laws than in anything resembling a democratic sentiment of mutual social support. Have these issues featured in your programmatic discussions?

Let me begin with a general observation. The economic recovery which was achieved in the 1930s by rearmament must be brought about, this time, by increased expenditure on social provision. If you re-equip industry you might achieve a shorter working week, because the microchip can revolutionize production. But microchips cannot revolutionize the care of the old or the young. There is a very big labour-intensive sector to be built up here, both to meet existing need and also as an instrument for achieving full employment.

Labour's programme goes into great detail about needs and how they might be met. Our main concern includes a range of measures to deal with the gap between rich and poor – which continues to widen – and measures designed to eliminate the inequalities experienced by women and by households which do not conform to the nuclear family. We have also looked at the question of the accountability of the social services, because we must get away from the harsh, poor-law type of administration that is now returning.

The Civil and Public Servants Association, which has now elected a left-wing leadership, has introduced a new element into the argument about social provision. The new generation of social-service workers – who are belittled by the right as 'the polyocracy' and so on – are becoming a major influence in the trade unions, and are beginning to take up on the industrial level the arguments that we are opening up for political debate, as well as responding to the manifest needs of the public in present conditions.

On the question of equal pay for women: the notion of 'equal work' has very widely been interpreted so as to frustrate progress towards equal pay. What measures would, or should be taken, in order to bring about a real and general advance towards equality in this area?

We recognize that the Equal Pay Act did not achieve the results that were intended, and that there is a limit to what can be done by legislation alone. Action on low pay gener-

ally, together with the development of women's demands by
the trade unions, seems to me very important now if there is
to be progress towards equal pay.

*What measures are envisaged for ending the oppression of
ethnic minorities — above all, blacks — in Britain?*

We have committed ourselves clearly to something we prom-
ised but never did: repeal of the 1971 Immigration Act and a
totally non-discriminatory immigration policy. We are working as closely as we can with the minority communities to
deal with some of the issues of discrimination. Unemployment has seriously threatened the black community, and our
urban renewal programme, which must be part of the systematic process of regenerating the economy, is going to
play a big role here. We are beginning to win the confidence
of the black community, though they have some reason to be
suspicious of the Labour Party, given its past record. The
process of getting these issues raised, and giving them their
due prominence, hinges on the extent to which we can per-
suade the ethnic communities that we are an instrument
worth using, even though they will still want to organize
outside the party as well.

*There are two specific reforms that should be relatively
straightforward for a Labour government: the institution of a
policy of affirmative action throughout its own area of employment, i.e. the state sector; and decisive measures against the
racist ethos of large sections of the police force.*

To take the second point first – proper police accountability
to elected authorities is the most important thing. We also
have proposals about the rules now governing arrest and
detention, and about the problem of racism in the police
force. On the question of affirmative action, we have made a
start in discussing positive discrimination in the party itself.
There are many people in the Labour Party who have not
regarded this as an important question, just as before the

First World War there was a principled objection in some sections of the party to votes for women. But the case for affirmative action is now being strongly made by the women's movement.

The Common Market

You said earlier that the AES was incompatible with continued membership of the EEC. Let's return to this question now. It has been said by very many people on the Labour left — and Michael Foot is particularly prone to make this claim — that British liberties are somehow of a different character, altogether superior to those enjoyed by our Continental cousins, and for this reason the EEC is essentially an unwelcome intrusion. But there is another argument, which is that the EEC institutions are fundamentally anti-democratic and bureaucratic, and affect all the member states equally. These two arguments have quite different political connotations and implications.

When I was president of the EEC council of energy ministers for six months in 1977, I used to sit and look at my colleagues round the table. Except for the Irish, who have a rather special attitude towards us anyway, I was the only minister there who had not lived under fascism or Nazism or been occupied by the Germans. For them the EEC represents an incredible liberation from a memory of oppression and war, while for us it was a derogation of our historic democratic right to select and remove our governments, which I don't think you should dismiss as unimportant. Democracy in Europe has grown and developed in a different way. France is a highly centralized state deriving from the Napoleonic period, and the French left is very much more highly centralized than the left in Britain. The role of the first secretary of the French Socialist Party compared with that of the general secretary or even the leader of the Labour Party is far more powerful in terms of the selection of candidates and the development of policy. We have this very strong radical tradition of local initiative – that's why the Tatchell affair has been so important – and this obstinate dissenting view has given a distinctive flavour to British democratic practice. In Germany democracy and trade unionism were an artificial implant after the defeat of Hitler. So you can look around and see very different national traditions in each case. All of us, however, are now subordinated to the Treaty of Rome, which is as hostile to the long-term interests of labour in Germany and France and Italy as it is in Britain. These are different arguments for repealing the Treaty – they overlay each other but they are different. I would not want to underestimate the potential for change that exists in the British parliamentary system, combined with a strong trade union movement, with all its weaknesses. I think you have to warn people that as well as the unfinished business of our own national development, there are now new EEC controls upon our democratic system and that the people's rights have been yielded to others who are not accountable to anybody.

But Britain's historic alternative wasn't really any kind of independence. What preceded the orientation towards the EEC was the 'special relationship' with the USA: it was North Atlantic politics. Isn't there a latterday equivalent of the 'Norman yoke' theory current in the Labour left, 'the Brussels yoke', and doesn't it involve a similarly unarguable version of British history and society? We've already seen that the constitution is a very effective apparatus of expropriation of popular sovereignty. Where is the qualitative difference of EEC membership?

I don't disagree with that. But the point I am really making is this, that with all its weaknesses, all its unfinished business, and all its 'special relationships', there was a potential for democratic and socialist development within a pre-Common Market Britain that is not present now. And it was the fear of this potential that turned the British Establishment towards the EEC. They saw in the EEC the ultimate constitutional safeguard against democratic socialism in Britain. The Foreign Office, a much more fearsome threat to the next Labour government than the Brussels Commission, now possesses an additional means of controlling us, as does the Treasury, and that new means is the Treaty of Rome. The real threat to the next Labour government, if we tried the AES, would be that, say, ICI would take us to the British courts alleging a breach of the Treaty, and the Lord Denning of the day would do to the cabinet what has been done to Ken Livingstone in London. The Brussels connection reinforces the anti-democratic obstacles in the constitution. I do not say that we cannot cooperate with Brussels, but I think we have to break with the Treaty of Rome. It is the very worst addition to the complications of our own inherited defects.

The Brussels bureaucracy as such is pretty puny, compared with national governments. It disposes of no armed force, and even its budgetary powers are quite limited. In this sense it is not a superstate, it is much less than a state. It can of course enhance the power of capital: there is free movement of capital itself, and this helps to discipline national working classes. The British bourgeoisie had strong economic reasons for favouring EEC membership, but as far as state coercion goes, Brussels does not count for anything.

It is certainly true that the Commission is made up of politically aware people who know that you cannot discipline a country the size of Germany or France or Britain. But I remember sitting in a cabinet committee where Sam Silkin, then Attorney General, announced that his brother, John Silkin, had broken the law on the pig-meat regime or something like that, and the committee immediately reversed its policy. Our instinctive obedience to the law was such that we behaved as though we had been caught on a double yellow line or with our hands in the till! I came to the conclusion – and to this extent I don't completely disagree with what you are saying – that a really determined British government that was not prepared to be put upon by the rather feeble attempt of the Commission to apply the Treaty of Rome, would make much more progress than we actually did. Nevertheless, I can visualize circumstances where the Treaty could activate all that is undemocratic in our own state. Say, for example, that a British-based company invoked one of its provisions against a Labour government measure, and that the British courts upheld the complaint. The measure would be ruled illegal, and the British civil service, having been advised that they could not break the law, would then say to the minister responsible: 'Your policy cannot be implemented'. At that stage we might try to repeal the European Communities Act. But if the House of Lords refused to cooperate, we would find ourselves in a constitutional crisis, and would be vulnerable to dissolution. I don't know what would happen then. I have spent a lot of my time thinking about how we might actually get out of a predicament like that.

Can you spell out concretely what AES-type measures would be obstructed by the EEC, because this is not so clear.

Let me take examples I know about from my own experience. The first was perhaps not of major importance but it revealed the mechanism. Heath introduced an interest relief grant scheme, under which industry in Britain could get a 3% reduction in interest rates for the manufacture of equipment for the North Sea oil field. This was to discourage every American oil company from buying every hammer and chisel back home in Houston or wherever, and as a result of this scheme and other measures we increased the proportion of British equipment used in the North Sea from 25% to 60%. However, I was summoned before three EEC commissioners and told that the scheme was illegal under the Treaty and that action would be taken against us. In the end the Commission decided to take us to the European Court – during the 1979 election, and the scheme was dropped by the Tories. The Treasury was glad to see the scheme go anyway, because it was expensive, and the Foreign Office didn't want to upset the Commission because it was trying to win some advantage or other at the time – that was that.

Of course the big issue was North Sea oil itself, because the applicability of the Treaty of Rome was uncertain here. Did it include those parts of the North Sea which, under the Continental Shelf Act 1964, were part of British territory, or only those within the twelve-mile limit? In the event of the Treaty being held to apply to the oil fields, then all sorts of consequences followed. It was argued that it was illegal to insist on the oil being landed in Britain; the Commission could insist on pipelines being laid straight to the Continent, which meant we would lose control of the trade in oil. The extent and rate of depletion of North Sea oil was subject to EEC agreements about the total net import of oil into the Community, within a general energy policy, and so on. The attempt to force a common nuclear power policy on us, which has been reinforced by the present government's decision to build the pressurized-water reactor, following the French and the Germans, was another instance of this kind of thing. Now, of course, it is true that we could have resisted all this and we did to some extent. I certainly resisted as hard as I possibly could where our interests were at stake. But EEC law is a lobster pot: you can get in very easily; but once you are in you can't get out because one veto can stop you. Gradually the whole of Common Market law, policy and philosophy begins to engulf the whole United Kingdom.

These are substantial matters. Looking forward, I think we would run into special difficulties if, for example, we tried to expand the steel industry contrary to the Treaty of Paris, which is much more federalist than the Treaty of Rome. Under Euratom, the EEC claims the right to buy all the uranium we have, and we are not now allowed to acquire our own uranium from Canada, Australia or anywhere else. The EEC claims the right of ownership of all uranium found in this country – this is clearly set out in the Euratom treaty – and a British trade policy for uranium would also be held to be contrary to the free movement of capital and goods. However weak it may be and however desirous of placating difficult countries, the Commission has the support of the bankers and the multinationals, who see in the EEC a powerful reinforcement of their resistance to interventionist or public-ownership policies in the United Kingdom. All this would be a barrier to us, and I am not yet persuaded that Mitterrrand will not, at a critical moment, be faced with some very strong EEC pressures, because he is not, in the end, exempt from such pressures

Shouldn't Labour then be developing links with the French left — be they with Mitterrand or with the Socialist Party, or with the Communists who may also be insisting on defence of the radical programme of their own government. Isn't this a priority for the British labour movement?

Yes, but I don't think that's a substitute for trying to get the constitutional position correct. Even if every single government in the Common Market were of the left, we – and they – would still be tied by the Treaty. The new Euro-socialist currents are very radical, and we should develop links with them. But the fact remains that we are landed with an obsolete constitution and a European legal structure that greatly reinforces its reactionary potential; and this makes for an extraordinary paralysis of socialist initiative. I went to the European parliament recently to talk to the socialist group about Labour policies, and my argument was: we are not anti-European, but the Treaty of Rome is an obstacle, and European socialists must accept that we will have to extricate ourselves from it. The Treaty is contrary to interests of the French, Italian and other European working-class movements as well as to the British. I think the European left is beginning to see this, and will see it even more clearly if Mitterrand is in any way frustrated, as I believe he will be in the end, by Brussels pressures. Then I think you might be quite surprised how rapidly our resistance to the Treaty will find allies on the Continent. That is not a nationalist view at all; it is the very opposite; it is an internationalist view based on the belief that for international labour to prosper, inter-

national institutions must reflect the interests of labour and
not those of capital.

Nuclear Disarmament

*One of the most welcome developments in British politics in
the last two years has obviously been the new and very powerful upsurge of CND and the rebirth of unilateralism in the
Labour Party. But a big question is posed here. When you've
been asked why the Labour Party has been doing poorly in a
whole series of by-elections you've said that one of the great
difficulties, perhaps the greatest difficulty, is that electors
don't know exactly where the Labour Party stands on many
issues. Now, let's assume that the commitment to unilateral
nuclear disarmament is enshrined in the party's manifesto. It
still is the case that leading members of the parliamentary
party, including virtually a majority of the shadow cabinet,
have publicly announced their unwillingness to think about
this policy, and there seems very little likelihood at the
moment that proportions can be so changed that there would
be a unilateralist majority in the PLP after the next election.
In these circumstances, posing the question simply as a potential Labour voter, with what degree of confidence can one
possibly look forward to a Labour government actually
renouncing nuclear weapons, with all that implies?*

My first answer would be that all change begins at the bottom and finishes up at the top. The last place I would expect
recognition of the need for change to occur in any organization is at the top, because the people at the top are by
definition part of the status quo. There are different cycles of
change, and you've got to watch all of them. The cycle of
change in public attitudes to nuclear weapons is very far
advanced. So much so indeed that we may even see the
beginnings of a new all-party opposition to the bomb. Within
the Labour Party the critical policy discussion is now in train.
Last year was partly dominated by the deputy leadership
election and the issues could be presented in terms of per-

sonality, but this year the focus is clearly on policy, on Labour's programme. I shall be participating in those discussions with a keen desire to answer your question: will I be able to go to my constituents next time and say, 'If you vote Labour the Trident will be cancelled, Polaris and Chevaline will be phased out, the US and British bases will go'? I hope that this year the Labour conference will accept full unilateral nuclear disarmament. But having said that, I believe that much remains to be discussed. We've been a bit slow in working out what we mean by non-nuclear defence. There's a lot more work to do on the NATO link and how far it could or should be retained, a lot more on END and the idea of a European nuclear-free zone. However, in these areas too things are moving rather more rapidly than I expected.

The main anxiety about a prospective Labour government is this. It would indeed cancel Trident — after all Denis Healey is against that, as indeed is Roy Jenkins. We could take it for granted that Chevaline would be wound down and Polaris phased out. But the really critical issue here is the American bases, and on this issue the leader of the Labour Party systematically evades public questioning. It looks very much as though what is being prepared is a position essentially similar to Bevan's. You can easily imagine the argument: we want to enter into a negotiating process with our European allies; we need time for this, and we would weaken our position were we to make any precipitate unilateral move. Etcetera. . . And so matters would be deferred indefinitely.

Well, you are fully entitled to raise any doubts you like until the manifesto is drawn up and you know how people respond to it. We will know soon enough. We are fortunate in one respect: President Reagan, with a dangerous and irresponsible policy that many people of all parties have now seen to be very frightening, is actually creating support for what we're saying. The way to get rid of the bases would be this. A minister would go to Washington the day we were elected to say that we were not prepared to have US nuclear, chemical or biological weapons placed in Britain or in our territorial waters, or flying over our airspace. The Americans would respond by appealing to existing agreements between the two states. We would then propose the publication of the agreements, so everybody could see them. That would be exceedingly interesting. We would allow about a year for withdrawal – as De Gaulle did in 1966 – and would insist that the weapons not be used during that period. Second, we would state our intention to legislate at the end of the period to make it contrary to domestic United Kingdom law for them to remain, and people who are now protected by the Visiting Forces Act from the application of domestic law would no longer be exempt. That's a very hardline position. What would happen if we acted on it? I think we would have enormous public support, once people understood the reality of the agreements secretly entered into by previous governments, including Labour governments.

Now whether the manifesto would spell this out, I do not know. But there is a general question here concerning the proper role of the party when Labour is in government. The more I reflect on this the more it seems to me very important that the party, while giving its support to the continuation of the government, should be concerned with advocating and further developing existing party policy. The pressure must be maintained throughout. We couldn't have more favourable circumstances for the discharge of that particular commitment than we have at the moment: a big CND, an extremely dangerous American president, and growing realization that in the guise of defending ourselves from a foreign power we're actually investing enormous power in our domestic military and in a resident foreign force – all to the disadvantage of our capacity for self-government. The issue is democracy as well as peace.

In effect you're saying that the present staunchly pro-American majority of the PLP, which would form the parliamentary basis of the Labour government, could be expected in some two years' time to have changed its mind

*under the pressure of popular opinion and the formal com-
mitment of the Labour Party conference. That you think is a
plausible perspective?*

Well that's the way it works – you've got to be realistic about
it. I hope that MPs will accept the manifesto. This is going to
be a very big issue in the election, and if a majority of the
next PLP were to frustrate the policy, they would be re-
versing a major public commitment.

The Falklands War

*The general debate over the risks of nuclear war has been
sharply punctuated by Britain's conventional war in the South
Atlantic. You were a prominent opponent of the military
expedition to the Falklands. What is your overall estimate of
the episode, and where do you think Britain now stands in
consequence of it?*

Nothing that has happened has altered my view that this was
a tragic and unnecessary war; and now that people are no
longer actually dying in battle, perhaps a somewhat calmer
atmosphere will allow an examination of the whole affair.
The unresolved issue of the Falklands led to armed conflict
after a period when diplomatic negotiations could have settled it completely. Had the government's ceasefire proposals
(which it later withdrew), for a United Nations trusteeship
under Argentinian and British observation, been put forward at any other time in the past twenty years, the whole
dispute would have been ended.

The eventual resort to arms raises a series of questions. It
has highlighted the world arms trade as a factor in world
politics. Argentinian ships were still in Portsmouth as
recently as a few months before the war, and a consignment
of spare parts was sent to the junta at a time when the risk of
an attack was manifest. We also need to ask how it was that
Britain began with the UN security council unanimously in
its favour and ended up with the security council unanim-

ously against it. What was it that we did, and at what cost? Then there is the question of the American role in the conflict. Washington supported Britain for a variety of reasons which will become explicit in time, but very unenthusiastically, because Mrs Thatcher has seriously damaged the political structure on which the USA rests in Latin America. The Americans will of course try to retrieve their position. They will press for Argentinian involvement in the future of the islands, which Mrs Thatcher cannot permit until after the next general election. Then the whole process will begin again.

What, then, was the cost of this useless exercise? Roughly 1,000 lives were lost. The financial cost of the fighting is already very great, and will continue to rise as long as the government persists in trying to secure the islands by maintaining a strong garrison there. Then there is the damage done to Britain's interests. This is where the Foreign Office will come back strongly: with 17,000 British people living in Argentina and £5 billion in investments there, any serious examination will show that the war was extremely damaging to British capital. In addition, you have to count the cost to our domestic political life: the use of war by an unsuccessful prime minister as a way of stimulating domestic support, and the way in which the media reacted, becoming in effect the mouthpieces of the ministry of defence. A tension has built up between the media and the government which will have to work itself out in some way, because there is no doubt that there was very tight censorship. And the appalling performance of Fleet Street's sewer press has had more than one kind of impact. War may begin with jingoism – the flags flying and the troops waving as the QE2 leaves Southampton – and this may be repeated when the survivors come home, but war agitates people in the sense of making them think. There was a lot more serious political discussion in those ten weeks than the media allowed us to know about; and impatience with Thatcher's uncompromising determination to win that war compared to her government's neglect of domestic problems could help create a different political perspective for Britain, if correct leadership is given. The moral and political vacuum that opened up in the House of Commons during this critical period is going to damage the Labour Party. It's going to damage people's confidence in the political process. The disillusionment of the public will grow quite sharply and quickly, and people will ask themselves, 'Well, what really happened?', and unless we've offered a consistent analysis, it may be that they will draw the conclusion that a more aggressive stance is the correct one. The rejection of international action by the prime minister – her contemptuous references to the UN – has done great damage to the prospects for peaceful settlement of international disputes.

You speak of a 'vacuum' in the House of Commons, but it wasn't really that. In effect the large majority of the PLP rallied to the war. You were among the small minority who stood out against it. What you're saying is that the principal alternative to the government, the leadership of the PLP, has been found grievously wanting in this episode. They weren't alone in this, of course. No doubt you're right that there was a great deal of discussion in the labour movement that the public has not been told about, but, important as it was, opposition to the war was generally weak.

I'm not sure that I accept that last point. Normally the balance of my correspondence is quite close to the balance of 'public opinion'. In this case it was heavily against the war. So I'm not persuaded that the public did support the war. Coming to your first point, I think that the process of transforming Labour opinion, even in parliament, was already under way by the time of the British landings. 83 MPs signed the ceasefire resolution: that's about one-third of the PLP, quite a substantial number. Many other MPs used to say at party meetings, 'Just wait, it will all go wrong and then we can criticize'. That was a completely opportunistic view, but it didn't indicate real support for what was going on. Of course the Labour Party itself was in a peculiar position:

during the municipal elections local party discussions were suspended, so that resolutions were late in coming through. But when they did come through they were overwhelmingly against the war. The women's conference in Newcastle passed a resolution condemning the dispatch of the taskforce, and the party conference in the autumn will assert itself very strongly. In response to the question, 'Why did the PLP act as it did?', I take a very broad historical view. The House of Commons is always the last place to get the message. New thinking always begins outside and filters in. The trouble is that in a sudden crisis the time for that process of popular correction of representative error doesn't correspond to the timescale of events, and so you get a period of error such as we've seen in this case.

CND did quite early on take a position against the war. Do you think that will undermine its support?

No, quite the reverse. There was anxiety lest the June 1982 CND demonstration would be reduced in size because of the war, but it wasn't. Not every CND supporter wanted to be diverted into the Falklands crisis, but it was very important that on this occasion, unlike say the Boer War or Suez, the peace movement was already in being, and it had a profound effect. One of the lessons of this war, relevant here, is that nuclear weapons are useless and conventional weapons are deadly. These two things have emerged out of the actual experience of the fighting, and they interact very directly with the analysis of CND.

You say that the war has somewhat undermined the UN and an international approach to settling conflicts among states. Has it not to some extent also increased the danger of military interventions by the First World in the Third World? Hasn't it changed the situation that appeared to exist at the end of the Vietnam War where the advanced states of Western Europe and North America were loath to undertake military expeditions in the Third World?

Yes, that's one effect; the second is the proposal for a South Atlantic treaty organization involving Chile, Argentina, the United States and South Africa. On the other hand, the picture of Costa Mendes hugging Castro in Havana, at the conference of non-aligned countries, opens up a different prospect for Third World development, and I'm not at all sure that the line-up of rich, militaristic capitalist countries against the developing countries won't be partly transformed by this. The temptation and the capacity to intervene may be greater, and successful interventions may occur, but the impact on Third World opinion would be tremendous. We would pay a very heavy price in the long term.

You've used a phrase that puts into question some of your descriptions of Britain. You sometimes depict Britain as being almost a semi-colonial country, dominated by the multinationals, by the EEC, by NATO. But now you've included Britain among the rich, militaristic capitalist powers. Which is it to be?

My suggestion that Britain is a colony greatly upset some on the left; I've read more criticisms of that than of almost anything else I've ever said. But I adhere to that analysis. Even in the Victorian era workers in Britain lived as a subject people under the British Establishment. The theory that the working class benefited from Empire, or will now benefit from success in the Falklands, is totally false. We are the last colony in the Empire. Almost every other country has broken free, and we are left with this decaying Establishment. The British Establishment has consciously sought reinforcement for its power in the American bases, Common Market membership, and the IMF. It was so frightened by the potential impact of a strong trade-union movement with a political party and a socialist analysis that it decided to hand the keys of the kingdom to others, the better to control us. It is an indication of the strength of our socialist and democratic traditions that this had to be done. The analysis is complicated, I accept; but I adhere to the view that we need a national liberation struggle, because until we gain democratic control in our own society we're never going to be able to play a proper role in World affairs. We must devote attention to our own domestic situation if we're going to be more than just one of the subject territories of an interconnected economic, political and military structure that has been set up as the long-term response to the forces released in the world by the Russian Revolution. To that extent, we have a common interest with those in struggle in the Third World.

Out of the Crisis

How would you summarize the British crisis as a whole, and the necessary response of a future Labour government to it?

I don't want to fall into the old trap of pronouncing on 'what's wrong with Britain'. But I think it's absolutely clear that it's a crisis of the British establishment, brought on by their failure to make their institutions and their values acceptable to the majority of the population by meeting its needs. There is nothing wrong with the British people that prevents them from coping with their problems. A baby chicken, before it is born, begins to peck away at its shell and many cracks appear; but what is giving way is only the shell, what is coming out is a new life. I think you've got to be very clear that what we're witnessing are the signs of birth, not the funeral of our people. The British working class has been persuaded by the media and the establishment not only that they caused the crisis but that they have earned the punishment they're getting, so the message that you have to spread is one of hope and confidence. Confidence is of critical importance. Fears are engendered by the last efforts of a defeated Establishment to impose itself against the emergent confidence of the British people, who are now better educated, who've got better communications despite all the weaknesses of the media, and have a real awareness growing within them of what they are capable of, even though they don't connect their present problems with the system under which they live. Labour governments can do an awful lot, but they will succeed only in so far as they help to crack that shell and let the new life out. It isn't so much what any government is going to do *for* us but what it can help us to do for ourselves. Meanwhile, what also matters is how far we can, here and how, campaign to build up demands and help to make them effective.

4
Labour and Socialism

We've discussed a large number of issues that now face the Labour Party — and that would become its direct governmental responsibility should it win sufficient parliamentary strength at the next election. But the party itself has become an issue of a very potent kind for British politics. The campaign of democratization inside the party has repeatedly been criticized by its centre and right opponents on the grounds that it has weakened Labour's function as an effective opposition and prospective alternative to the Conservatives. And sympathetic observers of the campaign — indeed many participants in it — now take the view that the period ahead must be devoted to the formulation and propagation of policy. This is understandable. But the process of democratization has its own dynamic; not all the issues have been settled and others remain to be posed. Besides, the prospects for Labour depend to a very large extent on the kind of party, the kind of political force, that it will from now on be. What in your view are the outstanding problems in this respect?

Let's be clear about what happened in the seventies, and particularly from 1979 onwards. I suppose it was the vote of seventy-odd Labour MPs against the three-line whip in the Common Market debate in 1971 that started the pressure for democratic change in the party. Then, in May 1973, Wilson vetoed the proposal to nationalize the 25 companies; and finally Callaghan vetoed the abolition of the Lords on the night of 2 April 1979, when we were discussing a first draft of the manifesto. Those were the three events that really fuelled the demand for democratic reform. As I said earlier, democracy is always a secondary issue: people think about it in relation to what's happened to them. ' We're in the Common Market, we've lost our socialist policy, and we're not allowed to have a democratic parliament. Why?' And that's the question that brings them to the democratic case. Given the fact that we'd been in power from 1964 with only a short break and were then beaten into the ground, 1979 was the right moment to raise these questions; all that pent-up feeling that had been held back by loyalty to a Labour government – and which, incidentally, kept me from resigning from the cabinet – was suddenly released. Although much of the public comment in the next two years was about the democratic changes, the really important policy changes were made in parallel: we got new policies on nuclear weapons, on economic strategy, and on Europe. Policy changes without the democratic reforms would've been meaningless; the socialist policy would hever have been implemented. The deputy leadership election became a sort of focus in which both were tested, with interesting results; overwhelming support from the constituency parties, a lot of trade-union support, and a very close outcome.

That ended one phase, and I think it was right for it to end then, in terms of priority because the price paid in public support for having a good look at ourselves was, it could be argued, that meanwhile we were not really engaged in the historic function of an opposition: to expose the government and to replace it. That certainly created unease and uncertainty (I'm not talking about the SDP secession because I think they would have gone anyway, having lost the battle in the party). It created a situation where we were really opening the way for a very destructive backlash from the party right, which is now taking place. Towards the end of 1981, without anybody writing anything down, it became clear to the left that there was now the basis for beginning the election campaign. We had good policies; we were not proposing to advance or to retard the democratic changes as a priority, although no doubt resolutions would go forward; there were not going to be expulsions – on his basis people would now pull together. That was the framework of the Bishop's Stortford meeting, even though the right later went back on it all.

Of course, the democratic changes themselves entail continuing processes. Reselection will begin again immediately after the next election; and the electoral college, had it been available to us at the time would certainly have stopped Wilson in his tracks on *In Place of Strife* and would have stopped Callaghan's 5% pay policy, because the possibility of a contest against the prime minister of the day would have had, and will have, a very profound impact. So we have made really important changes in the structure of the party, with lasting effects. However, there's a great deal more to be done, and when the time comes we'll take it up again. Greater democracy in local government – we still haven't made the changes necessary there. The issue of control of the manifesto will remain until it is resolved. There should be greater democratic control by the PLP within itself. Then, recorded votes: we need these for everything, not just for the deputy leadership election. This should be extended to all block votes, to NEC elections, and so on. We need to explore whether there aren't ways of developing democratic control of Whitehall. MPs must have a larger role in controlling the civil service. So this democratic argument isn't in any sense over. But I think our priority now, quite properly, must be to get across to the public the relevance of our policies to their needs. The democratic campaign is, I would say, suspended but still very much on the agenda, and I would expect it to be resumed after the next election – and meanwhile we must resist the drive for expulsions in the party.

Two specific questions, then, the first concerning the position of women in the Labour Party. At the minute a highly anomalous system prevails whereby the representation of women on the NEC — and if there is specific provision for women it's certainly very far from being an equal provision —

Labour and Socialism   113

is controlled by the conference at large, which means by the very large block vote of the unions, themselves massively dominated by men. Surely this cries out for speedy remedial action.

Reform of the NEC has been much discussed; it isn't a perfect system. I might add that, given the fact that the affiliation fee for a trade union is now 45p per member and the contribution for an individual party member is £6, it would be very much better if voting at the conference were on a 50/50 basis as between the unions and the CLPs, and of course that would reflect itself in the composition of the executive. Various proposals have been put forward; one is that five women should be elected by the women's conference. Though I am supporting this proposal, I am slightly nervous, perhaps for obscure constitutional reasons, of a composite executive that is not accountable to annual conference. The great thing about the executive is that when it goes to conference it meets its electorate. Even the leader and deputy leader meet their electorate there as they never did before, when they were visitors ex officio. If we did go for the basic 50/50 then we could have reserved seats for women in each section, elected by women.

You've already raised the second question, which relates to trade-union representation at the party conference. One way of pointing it might be to ask whether it is fair that the vote of a committed individual member of the Labour Party should be given no more weight than that of a trade union member who has never actually taken an active decision to belong or to pay dues to the party, and may indeed vote Tory?

The 50/50 ratio would deal with that: you see it would be a form of financial voting on the very rough and ready assumption that you have 6 million affiliated trade unionists paying 45p each and 600,000 members of the party paying £6. That would be fairer, but you've got to be very careful that you don't accidentally separate the Labour Party from the trade-union movement. I believe that the combination of a very powerful industrial movement with a political voice in parliament offers us the only practicable chance of mobilizing enough strength to change the balance of power in society as a whole. I don't want to do anything that weakens this link.

Within your perspective of change, wouldn't it be natural for the constituency parties to have their own conference, just as the TUC has its conference?

Well, it's not a strict parallel, because the TUC includes a lot of non-affiliated unions. But there is a history to all this. Up until the 1930s the whole conference voted for the constituency section of the NEC. There was no constituency section as such, elected by the CLPs, and it was the secretary of my local party, Herbert Rogers, who helped form the constituency parties association, which had a conference and succeeded in extracting the seven constituency members from the conference vote as a whole. There is a closer parallel: Trade Unions for a Labour Victory – which is actually not an affiliated-trade-union conference, because it never meets as a conference. The general secretaries of affiliated unions (with one or two exceptions, including the miners) get together. It is potentially open to the constituency Labour Parties to set up a 'CLPLV'. I think there are certain dangers in all this because I don't want to disaggregate the party. But the Campaign for Labour Party Democracy has given a greater sense of identity and common purpose to the constituency parties than they had before; and the deputy leadership election created an enormous interest in, and awareness of, the potential of the constituency parties. Previously they had never been allowed to play a role at all in the election of the party leadership.

You talk about the complexity of these proposals for democratizing the labour Party. Isn't there a risk now of a sort of complacency about structures that remain undemocratic and frustrating for the ordinary socialist militant. The situation is such that the real members of the party have only a 10% say in its deliberations. And you were defeated in the deputy leadership election although you won well of 80% of the votes of the real members of the party, the constituency section. Isn't it a matter of burning urgency that Labour should acquire an internal structure that gives a more authentic reflection of what the real party workers and activists would like, in leadership and in policy? Isn't there a real danger that the Labour Party may not overhaul itself democratically in time to remain a really major, serious political force?

The continued democratic development of the Labour Party is very important. We must keep up the flow of interpretation and under standing so that people never lose sight of the issues altogether. I think it's much too early to say that we're becoming complacent. At this moment we have just completed a full programme that fleshes out what conference wants; we must now step up the campaign to get rid of the government and elect a majority Labour government. I'm satisfied that we've done the right thing in making that our priority in 1982.

The New Political Campaigns

Many people would say that the Labour Party has become very decrepit as a political machine and no longer has the capacity to win a majority for the sort of policies you've been talking about. Just compare it with other workers parties in Europe, with their strings of local newspapers, large and vital women's and youth movements, and so on. Does Labour really show the will to liberate the energies of its own members, to allow its constituency parties to grow and take on new tasks — for example, to publish newspapers in the big cities?

We are very short of money. Many of the continental parties get state aid, which is a two-edged weapon. The constituency parties are active, and their membership is slowly growing,

despite the swingeing increase in subscription rates. Our
youth movement is active, and our women's movement has
undergone a major change in the last two to three years,
becoming much stronger and much more radical. We must
not speak as if the party was on its last legs, but clearly it has
a lot more to do – the development of factory branches, for
example, which has been agreed in principle but not really
done in practice. Many party branches publish news-sheets
of one kind or another – far more than you might think – but
none of them has the resources to produce a local paper.

*Yet the party puts hundreds of thousands of pounds into
advertising campaigns at each election . . . .*

That may be so. I opposed the £90,000 spent on public opinion polls in the last election: it would have been much better
used somewhere else. And it is certainly arguable that
instead of major advertising campaigns it would be wiser to
try to fund a better distribution of published material, but it
would still be very much on a one-off news-sheet basis.
Though if we got a launch fund going for our media proposals then we would really be in business: there would be the
possibility of minority papers, including socialist papers,
being catered for. You've put your finger on some very
important organizational problems; the Labour Party is still
a relatively small organization – and a lot of our strength and
muscle comes from our organic link with the trade unions
who, with mass unemployment and the Tebbit legislation,
are turning increasingly to political action, as you would
expect, when they find themselves hamstrung by economic
weakness on the industrial front.

*You mention the importance of the trade-union link. We're
living through an unprecedented attack on welfare and educational provision, and one consequence of Labour's programmes in the past is that there are many, many employees in
this area in the trade union movement. This has been one of
the big areas of growth for the unions and it's been a strength*

for the left within the Labour Party, on the whole. Yet to date
these unions have been a little too defensive, too narrowly
concerned with their corporate interests. Is it not the case that
the more generous, socialist aspirations you were describing
earlier would actually require a tremendous development of
these welfare and educational agencies; and shouldn't these
unions, which historically have prided themselves on being
outside politics, be plunged into *politics in a new way?*

Yes: the ASTMS for example, is a pretty imaginative and
go-ahead union; and NUPE, which is growing quite rapidly,
has taken a very broad view of its responsibilities. The
TGWU campaigned very strongly on pensions. So things are
moving; but remember that overhanging the whole of our
society is fear, and fear is affecting everybody including the
labour movement. It certainly makes thoughtful people dig
deeper down, but it's only when hope begins to appear again
that new ideas spread. I wouldn't underestimate the potential for rapid development, but at the moment we really are
in a siege. People are defending their capacity to survive, let
alone to work, to be educated, and to retire in dignity. And
that reflects itself in the caution that surrounds so much
trade-union activity.

This brings us to the relationship between the labour move-
ment and other social categories. Could it not be said that
Labour, at least as it is now organized, doesn't have the capac-
ity to project and popularize a general *political and social*
alternative? It remains very much a corporatist, union-based
party, and is not instinctively seen by, say, black British
people, or by many Scottish workers, or many women work-
ers, as the repository of a programme of liberation for them.

I accept that we still have a disunited working-class movement, for some of the reasons you give, and others. It is a
movement with powerful trade-union representation but
with defects in its internal democracy. It is still very uncertain about its socialism, and still hasn't established proper

relationships with the women's movement, the black movement, the peace and ecology movements. The sense of oppression shared by the overwhelming majority of people in Britain has to be analysed and clarified, and tackled in education, campaigns and struggles.

Within that political perspective there are at least two broad options for Labour. One is that the party, through programmatic development, might become rich enough and capacious enough to absorb, in the benign sense, these various movements. Do you envisage the development of Labour politics as having that consequence? Or is it a matter of the party discovering forms of practical alliance with movements that would remain independent of the party?

That is a very interesting way of putting the question. What is the future structure of the relationship between the party and the unions – which are both male-dominated and largely white – and other movements? There must be a new and different working relationship between the party and unions and all the elements that would need to be assembled in order to end the rule of capital and open the way for change. But that does not mean that these movements should join the Labour Party and dissolve their own campaigns. Our main affiliated organizations, the trade unions, regard their link with the party as secondary and additional to their prime purpose. What brings miners together is their class interest in mining: in the conditions of mining work, in the living standards of miners and their communities, all of which also creates the need for a political voice. But miners are primarily interested in mining, and in the same way feminists are primarily interested in the problems facing women. Many of the issues confronting the women's movement have little to do directly with the ownership of capital but relate to other social structures. For a long time I have urged that we should reopen the party's affiliation list, so that the women's movement, the Indian Workers Association, the ecology movement, and so on, could affiliate as the unions have done. This would not mean that they would abandon their own battles, any more than the miners have abandoned theirs. All affiliated organizations would be free to develop the policies they need as the unions do. But all this argument and activity would also feed into the party, with dramatic results. Imagine a Labour conference where the women's, peace and ecology movements enjoyed a voting power in proportion to their membership. This would transform the party, which is one reason why the party is so reluctant to open itself to these influences. In the end many activists in these movements will conclude that only by affiliating will they be able to develop their own particular campaign into decisive political action. This perspective is not only electoral; it also encompasses the working relationship of the labour movement to those in struggle now. We are naturally preoccupied with the development of policy – what is the next Labour government going to do? But we cannot know when 'the next Labour government' will be there to do anything. Meanwhile what do we do *now*? Life is about here and now; some people living and suffering today will be dead before the next election, whoever wins it. So we must begin to develop forms of practical solidarity with struggles as and when they occur. A new alliance must be brought into being, indeed is coming into being – though our taskforce will take longer to assemble than that for the South Atlantic.

What would be the real basis for this alliance? A characteristic feature of the movements we've been discussing, including the unions, is what Raymond Williams has called 'militant particularism': they organize around their own oppression, separately and often narrowly considered. Surely it's not enough to say that their common basis is that in some undefined way they are all fighting capitalism. Isn't the British state itself one tangible common oppressor against which all these movements could begin to unite in a politically lucid and cohesive way?

'Militant particularism' is too narrow a characterization.

The awareness of opression, the decision to fight it, the thought-processes that those struggles encourage and the political perspectives that develop through them—this is what will hold the alliance together. It is in part an alliance against oppressive state power, for a democratic state – and the opening up of a debate about the nature and role of the state has been of the greatest importance for the left. But it is also a struggle for greater equality in income and services.

If socialists in the Labour Party are to build real relationships with these various particular struggles and to develop a general socialist vision that really establishes the common, or the compatible, interests of these movements, there will obviously have to be fundamental progammatic advances. But the actual practice of the party as a political organization will have to change too. This seems an unresolved problem for at least some on the Labour left. You find dedicated activists and representatives with quite new policies but with a relatively unreconstructed political practice whose focus is too narrowly on elections and on the activity of the representative chamber, be it local or national.

Yes, but do not underestimate what is being achieved. The strength of the left in the Greater London Council grew out of changes in party practice. *London Labour Briefing* began the process of explaining what was happening in the party, and what was the relationship between party practice and political effectiveness. The new left majority secured a great achievement in getting rid of the Conservative administration – and we must never forget the importance of removing from power those who represent another interest by an electoral victory. The GLC left then recognized that they couldn't succeed simply in the terms of County Hall activity, and they had to continue as a campaigning party. One example is to be found in the permanent display in huge figures on the roof of County Hall of the current unemployment rate for the Greater London area. In this and many other ways they opened up the communications battle. The GLC also launched a newspaper, *The Londoner*. The new low fares were very popular, and even when they were over-ruled the Labour GLC exposed the political bias of the judiciary. As for the fares campaign itself: the GLC was confined by the legal limits of municipal activity, and the trade unions were subject to the general fear that unemployment has created, so there was only so much they could achieve. But the London Labour Party has worked with the GLC leadership in a way that had never been seen before. The structures of the party changed in the process. Ken Livingstone and the Labour group are not a new establishment operating within the limits of the old. Practice has changed along with policy, even if the change won't show overnight results.

But the national picture is not so positive. There was a period when the party NEC was taking a lead in outward-going campaigns, but this appears to have ended.

There was a big political shift to the right in the NEC in 1981 and it was never 'left-dominated' as the media argued. The question we have to face is to what extent can we campaign for a better NEC, and to what extent would campaigns on inner-party matters expose us to the charge that we are alienating ourselves from the public. What the left should do now is to campaign for party policy in full view of the people. CND and even our anti-war campaigns prove that given a clear political initiative when it matters, you can get a response from the public.

There are relatively significant numbers of socialists who are not in the Labour Party. Many of these are not even prospective members, because they are already committed to other socialist organizations — the Communist party and the Socialist Workers Party being the two most prominent. Given that there is no plausible medium-term prospect that all socialist forces will be gathered inside the Labour Party, how do you think relations between socialists in the party and those outside it, whether they are organized or not, should develop?

I don't want to see the various schools of socialist thought close down. They are very valuable, and nothing should happen to prevent them contributing their independent analyses and critiques of Labour governments and of the party itself. However, during the Wilson and Callaghan years a lot of politically active people withdrew from the party because they believed that Labour, under its right-wing leadership would never achieve anything approaching socialism, and indeed would be an obstacle to realizing it. The fall in Labour party membership, as these people filtered into minor socialist groupings that were supposed to be alternatives to Labour, was very bad for us. That process of withdrawal has been largely reversed now. I would like individual socialists to join the Labour Party because their presence would be helpful, but I would not say that this is a necessity. If they are contributing to an *external* critique and are able to find relationships of intellectual discussion through an organization like the Socialist Society, that's well and good. What we have to prevent now is the *expulsion* of socialists from the Labour Party. The way we respond to the attack on the Militant Tendency is crucially important. Militant is not so very significant politically; its members are the fundamentalist evangelicals of the party, and as such they have a place in it. The attack on them is designed to intimidate the left as a whole. It is also an indication of continuing SDP influence: the torch of anti-socialist intolerance that Shirley Williams held aloft has now been handed to others still in the party. This attack will not succeed. The left has to explain that the new witch-hunt represents the continuing right-wing influence in the party leadership, and embodies the intolerance associated with the right. Both inside the party and outside, we want socialism to be seen as a mosaic and not a monolith.

But there have been occasions — not many, it's true — when sectors of the Marxist left were not just intellectual critics but had a real political capacity equal to or greater than that of Labour Party militants: in the Anti-Nazi League, for instance.

And there are people on the right of the Labour Party who not only want to sweep socialists of all stripes out of the party but regard even occasional practical relationships with other organized left forces as politically unacceptable. The question here is not one of discussion and criticism, but of socialist unity in action.

No doubt there will be an attempt by the right to break broad-left struggles as well, but that will be particularly difficult to do, given that the right wing of the party works with right-wingers in other parties. Local Labour parties would simply not accept a ban on left cooperation on clear issues like racism or nuclear disarmament. Of course Labour could not contemplate any electoral arrangement with parties that put up candidates against us. But broad-left cooperation in the trade unions or in, say, the Anti-Nazi League or Chile Solidarity is perfectly natural, and to force a break on that would be beyond the capacity of the right wing of the party.

You believe that the Labour Party is, or can be, the voice of British labour and of all socialism. But the party as such has never been socialist, and its internal procedures — above all the conference – remain very frustrating for socialists. Is there not something to be said for the course taken in other European countries, where groups of socialists have broken with the inherited structures of the labour movement to found new left parties? The Greens in West Germany and the PdUP in Italy are more than intellectual ginger groups — they have both an electoral and a campaigning capacity.

That may be an arguable proposition for those countries. I suspect that the Labour right would like to see the left leave as the ILP did in the thirties. It was also the strategy of the various 'external' lefts in the sixties and seventies, but I can't say that the record has vindicated that strategy. If, as you say, clear socialist politics could find a wide response, then we should channel this response into the Labour Party. Then our numbers will grow, and clear socialist politics will be correspondingly strengthened. The recruitment of new, young, socialists into the party in recent years bears this out. There is no reason, in my view, why we shouldn't succeed in re-converting the Labour Party to socialism. It will take time and effort but it can be done. The Labour Party was founded to advance socialism, and events have put socialism back on the agenda.

Common Ownership and Redistribution

We'd like to come to the wider question of what you yourself would mean by socialism. There are two sides to this question. The first is to what extent is socialism a negation, something different from the capitalist society we live in today. Clause Four of the party constitution enshrines a commitment to common ownership of the means of production, distribution and exchange, and forms of popular administration. The problem about this formulation is that it doesn't really specify how far this common ownership actually extends. In your conception of socialism, as a historical stage of society that we can envisage in the future, as something that we work towards, how much of production, distribution, exchange is in common ownership?

If you're asking me where we are ultimately going to end up, it's very hard to say. My belief, as a socialist, is that of the three centres of power now existing – ownership of capital, the organization of labour and the ballot box, the first should be replaced by the second and third, the ballot box and the initiative of labour. Then out of the interplay between the interests of labour – the working people and their families – and the expression of the interests of the community at large through the ballot box, a new constitutional settlement will emerge – an enhancement and development of the democratic system that will lift the burden of exploitation arising from capital and all that flows from the market forces it requires to survive. I see this as a process rather than as an end-point, the 'socialist commonwealth' of the 1945 manifesto. The route we take will depend partly on circumstances. If you get a major decline, as I think we now have, in the stability of the market system, then more people – if they move to the left, and that will only happen if they have a perspective, and fair media – would want to act quite rapidly to reduce the power of capital. The route would also be determined by the nature of the opposition. If as I believe, the major opposition to social change lies in what Bevan used to call 'the commanding heights of the economy' or what Stuart Holland calls '100 leading companies', then we would have to redefine the mixed economy in terms of size: the major companies would have to be owned or accountable to the community and the medium or small companies would then be seen as operating, as they now do anyway, in response to them. That redrawing of the public-private demarcation line sets an objective that would carry you through a whole parliament and more. I would hope we could go beyond that, because a shift in the balance of power within firms that are large but not dominant – small businesses are different – would really begin to replace market forces as the sole determinant of economic activity. Government initiatives would be in response to what one would call non-economic imperatives. People accept that the whole defence sector is outside the area of market forces because we must have defence, irrespective of commercial calculations. In the same way you would begin to apply social imperatives – production for need, better social services, and so on – in other areas of national life. Where this process ends up will depend on what people actually want. I would not like to say, *this* is how it's going to be. At the moment working people have very little power to shape their lives or the nature of their communities or the industries or firms in which they work. They are almost literally slaves within the system. The process by which we advance should give them the power to decide how *they* want it to be.

You've spoken of the 100 largest companies being taken into public ownership; would you regard that as something like a transition point. The reason for pressing the question is that there were many leading Labour politicians — most notably Tony Crosland — who claimed as early as the fifties that we were already living in a society that was no longer capitalist. It's very striking that the enemies of the left use the term socialism to denounce the Labour Party much more frequently than Labour representatives ever speak of capitalism. There are many people in the party who think it's not very good form to speak of capitalism. So the question of the point of transition is very important.

Yes, we have allowed the right-wing or capitalist or Tory definition of socialism to be hung round our necks. It isn't socialism, but it has silenced us on the subject of what socialism should be, and yours is a perfectly proper question to put. Crosland, of course, really did believe that the control mechanisms established partly by wartime and post-war planning and partly by the skilful fine-tuning of the economy (which he believed would be possible in the hands of a Labour Chancellor of the Exchequer) could maintain full employment forever; generating wealth in that way you could redistribute the surplus to enhance equality, and so the private ownership of the means of production became irrelevant – the more completely so since these were now controlled by professional managers who were basically citizens with a consumer orientation. That whole theory finally blew up in his face in 1976 – after the IMF blackmail. The expansion of common ownership using many forms to achieve it is a crucial part of a policy for socialism. But remember that we never have brought any industry into public ownership without the explicit demand of the unions representing the people who worked in the firm or industry concerned. Therefore to contemplate taking over 100 companies whether or not the people who worked in them really wanted that is a different matter.

But this is the question of making socialism a popular objective.

Yes it is and media bias makes it harder. It's partly that the right wing have managed to impose upon the public, and even upon us, the image of a bureaucratic, Gosplan-type socialism, which is actually foreign to what we want. But it lies within our power to change that. Let me give you an interesting example: a proposal to bring the whole nuclear industry into one publicly owned consortium. I insisted at one stage that there be an explicit inquiry into the views of the people who worked in the industry. When this was done it was discovered that a majority even of the upper management wanted to be brought into the public sector. I think there would be the same desire among a large number of people, provided they had an opportunity of hearing all sides of the argument fairly presented and determining the matter for themselves, and, second, that what they go into is different from a steel corporation under MacGregor or a railway board under Parker. Given this capacity to transform the nature of the relationship with their owners or managers, many workers would think seriously about whether it wasn't advantageous. We have grossly underestimated the potential of such a demand by never defending ourselves against capitalist assaults upon socialism and never thinking fundamentally about what we could actually do. Supposing we applied the constitutional mechanism of the ballot and said, 'All right, let's have a ballot on the ownership and control of this company', there would be a response provided the alternatives were not limited to the old type of nationalization. The real problem could be that we would end up with a serious investment strike – of a kind we have already experienced – which we would have to deal with by other mechanisms. So far we haven't even begun to open up these perspectives.

We're discussing preconditions for a socialist society rather than socialism itself. Now there's one aspect of this that was actually posed not long ago in your relations with the shadow cabinet, namely the question of compensation for the share-

holders of industries taken into public ownership. You have repeatedly stated that no Labour government would ever adopt an attitude of confiscation. But there is a fundamental logical difficulty here. If we envisage a socialist society as one in which there is common ownership of the means of production, distribution and exchange, how could we ever approach it or anything remotely like it if each time a major capitalist enterprise was nationalized the equivalent sum of capital was simply paid out to the former owners? Capitalism would simply be displaced, undiminished, into other sectors of the economy, and the proportions of private capital and public enterprise would never change. By respecting the principle of market evaluation, as Labour has done to date, you close the passage to a socialist society.

It's a little bit more complicated than you make out. Certainly the type of compensation paid – the term has always been 'fair' compensation – has been either on asset value or on share value, and the way in which that has been calculated has been over-generous, notably in the case of the pits where it became so outrageous that the government actually had to transfer the coal stock to the National Debt. If you look at the thinking of the Labour Party in the 1930s you'll find that the idea was to reduce the amount of compensation by all sorts of factors including the extent of previous government support and the amount of protection formerly afforded by quotas and tariffs. None of this ever really came out in the post-war years, and the compensation was indeed generous. Now *confiscation*, by Act of Parliament, has a very clear legal meaning: we would be taking the property and saying, 'From this moment this belongs to us'. Nobody could dispute its legality in domestic terms (thought its international legality might be more dubious), but one of the reasons against doing it would be that people would not think it was fair if we tried to act in this way, and we would never win the public support necessary to do it. So between the two you really are driven to a more rigorous examination of what compensation means and how you assess it. Now as

for the renationalization of the privatized elements of the
National Oil Corporation, the party conference declared
that we would pay no compensation. I lost my place in the
shadow cabinet because, in November 1981, I simply repeated that policy from the front bench. I explained at the time
that our specific policy of renationalization did not provide
for compensation as defined by custom and practice,
because we would be taking away the value accumulated
since privatization. I hinted in a *Guardian* article at the time
that there should be a special mechanism for determining
the amount to be refunded in cases where there is reversal of
privatization. In effect the affected parties would receive a
cash refund representing the real value of their outlay at the
time of privatization, but nothing more. This would not be
the same as compensation, but equally it would not be confiscation – which I don't think should be the practice of a
Labour government. Within a few months my refund proposal became official Labour and TUC policy.

*You say it would be unfair not to compensate. But surely part
of the basic socialist case against capitalism is that it is an
unjust social order and that the root of the injustice is that a
small minority is very wealthy, while a very large majority is
not at all wealthy, if not outright poor. That is, if you like, the
traditional Christian way of putting it; the more Marxist way
of putting it is to say that this small minority controls much
more than just private wealth; by its control of the means of
production it actually controls the lives of the vast majority.
That's not 'fair' by any definition. But if you are really going
to compensate in the strict meaning of the term, the rich will
go on being rich, and the poor will go on being poor, so
you're not going to effect that fundamental redistribution of
power and wealth of which you have so often spoken. It can't
be done.*

It's certainly true that if you analyse the behaviour of some
of the big companies that owned industries now nationalized, you'll see that they simply moved their cash into the

growth industries, leaving the nationalized industries to cope with the problem of decline. That is a perfectly fair point. If compensation were the only consideration then you could argue that it made no difference: but of course it is intended, isn't it, to be accompanied by a wealth tax and stricter death duties, which will eliminate some of these inequalities. I do not believe that the arbitrary confiscation of assets, which is what you are really arguing for, would be a viable political option to put before the electorate. However you argue it through, I do not believe that there is an alternative to some form of compensation, however paid, for duly acquired assets, combined with policies of taxation of one kind and another that deal with the accumulation of wealth that would persist after compensation had taken place. Certainly the Labour Party has never given thought to anything other than a strict interpretation of what can properly be called compensation.

All right then: why couldn't you simply set the amount of compensation at ten times the minimum wage in the industry concerned? If you stick to compensation by market value you disable yourself from ever making any kind of socialist case against capitalism. You can't say that capitalism is an unfair system, and then maintain that compensation by capitalist norms is fair. It's an absolute contradiction.

I take your point. But you are moving from the area of acquisition to that of taxation: if you have a tax system that lays down a 10:1 ratio of income and wealth overall, you are arguing a different case. That is the way I myself would look at it; death duties, wealth tax and income tax could effect substantial changes in the distribution of income, but it may be a mistake to link this to the criteria on which industry should be brought into public ownership.

All the previous attempts to use taxation for redistributive purposes have been spectacularly unsuccessful. Britain remains one of the most unequal capitalist countries in this respect.

But it is open to a determined government that really set itself the objective of substantially narrowing the gap between rich and poor to do a great deal more than has been done.

Say we accept your position: full market compensation, but on the other hand a wealth tax. Now you know that when the Labour Party has gone in for a wealth tax the media and the Tory party, the establishment, has cried havoc. More precisely, they cry 'confiscation!' A wealth tax is a form of confiscation. However you dress it up fiscally, if the rich have their riches taken away from them they are going to regard it as confiscation, so where's the real difference?

That is an argument that can be used both ways – for confiscating nationalization, or against a wealth tax! The defensibility of our policy may determine whether we are likely to be elected to carry it out, whether we are going to be sustained in doing it, and whether the policy is likely to be durable or not. I believe that it would be better to tackle the distribution of wealth and income as a problem in its own right rather than by the sheer chance of whether or not we were proposing to take over a particular company.

Socialist Horizons

We've so far been insisting very much on the economic preconditions for socialism, but clearly just taking large companies into the public domain is not itself a guarantee of a freer, more just, socialist society as traditionally conceived. What would be your major emphasis in giving a positive definition of a socialist society? This is something very much underplayed not only in the Labour Party's approach to the general public but on the left as a whole.

Clause Four is economically oriented in the main, but the idea of popular administration is also there, and it thus envisages the enrichment and enlargement of the democratic process, the transfer to people of the capacity to control their own lives, in the organizations where they are working or living, but also the capacity for much freer interpretation of their lives in society. Socialism inevitably means that production and services should be based on need rather than profit. But socialism also means trying to encourage people in the broadest possible sense, to draw out from them their full potential, which is enormously rich and varied. This is where even our limited educational reforms have been so absolutely successful in proving the potential for self-development on a scale that had never previously been thought possible. Our society, as it is now structured, consists still of a few individual successes built upon a pedestal of statutory failure – economic failure, educational failure, or failure of some other sort. The whole competitive idea that a nation must have so many failures in order to produce one success is ludicrous yet it is the foundation of capitalist ideology. Why do we describe so many people as having failed? Why are we not able to recognize that in any society the richest resource is people? Why is it that people, when they do have the free time now available to them – through a shorter working week or, worst of all, the enforced free time of unemployment – do not have the facilities for discovering the potential that lies within them? Asking questions like this, you come to realize that at the deepest level socialism must mean liberation.

Liberation is not just a question of doing what you like, because there is a socialist morality too, based upon the belief that no one should exercise their freedom in such a way as to introduce new exploitative relationships vis-à-vis others – partner, children, work-mates, community – or the world. Socialism cannot stop at the front door; it must enter into the home. And as the old, rigid, imposed church moralities begin to lose their hold on people, we will find that, far from having escaped all moral imperatives, we will rediscover a social morality through our relationships with other people and will come to terms with what that demands of us. There will also have to be some structure for resolving conflict on the basis of this different but extremely powerful self-imposed morality. This is very rarely thought about or discussed, but people do have some perception of it; otherwise they would not be excited by socialist imaginings. Perhaps the Jamaican PNP's definition, 'socialism is love', is relevant here. I find in talking to people that it is possible to sketch out a different type of society, unlocking enthusiasms and excitements that would certainly not be unlocked if we always defined socialism in terms of industrial restructuring or economic policy. This excitement may become real when people realize that it is the private ownership of capital that locks them up. Maybe the function of the economic aspects of socialism is to unlock all the cells in which we live. Then, all of a sudden, we may realize what we might be, what we should be, what we want to be. The narrowly economic view of socialism that we often project is itself one of the reasons why the right has been able to make socialism look so negative, so full of abolitions and restrictions and restraints, when it really ought to be, and could be, an experience of liberation. There are many visions of that liberation in the ecology movement, in the black movement, in the women's movement, and in the work of artists and intellectuals, who are very little understood, especially in this country. These people often do not recognize capitalism as the prison that confines them all; but all of them in their different ways dream of a decent socialist way of life. Their demands are often of a kind that no act of parliament alone could provide for. One of the general functions of a socialist economic policy would be to liberate our initiative, our capacity to develop, and to allow us to remake our lives for ourselves. This dream of real freedom is what inspires democratic socialists all over the world.